The Wind of Life
The Flyers

Oliver Neubert

Vancouver, Feb. 23. 2012

To Judy

Purple Branch Publishing

First Published in 2011 by
Purple Branch Publishing
Vancouver, BC, Canada

Neubert, Oliver 1961
www.oliverneubert.com

The Flyers / Oliver Neubert - 1st ed.
p. cm - (The Wind of Life trilogy; bk. 1)

[Fantasy, Fiction, Coming of Age, Life Skills, Adventure,
Justice, Relationships, Reluctant Readers, Family Issues,
First Love]

ISBN: Paperback: 978-0-9868525-0-3

ISBN: e-Book: 978-0-9868525-1-0

Cover Layout and Idea: Chantel Neubert
Reviewer: Samantha Starkey
Reviewer: Calum Macdonald
Editor: Marjorie Dunn
Cover Design: Accurance Group, Inc.
Book Design: Accurance Group, Inc.

The Flyers — Book 1

Places:

The Five Mountains:

Mountain of Glory: home of the Elders and the Library of Stones
Mountain of Clouds: location of the Meeting Hall of the Council and the fortress of the
War Flyers
Mountain of Sun: the training grounds for the Rescue Flyers
Mountain of Life: location of the Halls of Healing, a place of healing and bringing of life
Mountain of Wind: location of the villages, homes, fields and schools of all the Flyers,
and the Cliff

Other Places:

The Old Mountains: where life began
Ardar: the old, secret hiding place of the Rescue Flyers
The Flatlands: the land in front of the Mountains where the Wanderers live

Characters:

Three Elders:

Air: the oldest of the Elders, also known as the Seer
Wind: the wisest of the Elders, also known as the Wise One
Earth: the smartest of the Elders, also known as the Scientific One

Seven Lords:

Aldor: Lord of the Rescue Flyers
Wardor: Lord of the War Flyers
Dodor: Lord of the Healing Flyers
Stodor: Lord of the Storm Flyers
Raidor: Lord of the Rain Flyers
Wolf: Lord of Wolf Forest
Golden Eagle: Lord of the Sky, protector of the Mountain of Clouds

Three Young Flyers:

Timo: Fourteen years old, he has the gift and can hear the words of the Wind
Dino: Fourteen years old, Timo's best friend and future navigator
Val: Fourteen years old, Timo's classmate, she also has the gift and can see the future

Contents:

While you are soaring, enjoy the beauty around you, but do not be lost in the feeling of freedom and invincibility because the deadly cold downdraft is waiting for you in the thunderclouds.

Written by Gildor, Lord of the Rescue Flyers, from his book, *Soaring*, Chapter 10

CHAPTER ONE

The Cliff

The morning wind blew cold air across the high peaks of the five mountaintops, and the world of the Flyers was darker than ever before. During the night, rain had showered down like waterfalls. A white mist filled the valleys. Mud covered the ground and the tall trees stood like lost nomads in a strange land. Timo felt the cold downdraft in the air. This lifelong enemy had tried to break his wings several times. He was worried he wouldn't be able to overcome the downdraft this morning, but he had to try. The time had come to show everyone he was ready to join the Rescue Flyers.

"Let's get going," Timo whispered up to his friend's window. He was excited, nervous and impatient. The previous night had been painfully long, and he hadn't slept very well. Timo's naked feet had traveled silently across the wet grass towards his friend's house while the sun slept below the eastern horizon. Timo was ready. He moved his wings on his back smoothly, allowing warm blood to flow through the cold arteries that made his wing muscles move. The slight morning wind breathed through his curly hair and tingled his feathers. Timo tried to ignore his emotions. He had to focus on what he had to do. His heart was beating loudly and he thought the whole village could hear it, but everything remained still; even the baker's house showed no sign of life.

The small village that stood in the forest along the western side of the Mountain of Wind was silent and peaceful. Timo was starting to call it home, but this hadn't always been the case. He and his mother had moved to this place from the northern side of the mountain three years ago.

Suddenly, a tired face looked out of the window and a mellow voice said, "It's too early, Timo. The updraft isn't strong enough this early in the morning."

"By the time we reach the Cliff it will have picked up strength. We discussed this before, Dino," Timo urged. "Come on, you promised."

"I know I promised, but I am scared. What if we get caught? You know the penalty for flying down the Cliff if you are not a Rescue Flyer."

"We discussed all this before," Timo growled angrily. "Have you forgotten? I am the one who will do it, not you! I want to do it this early so no one will see us. Don't be afraid and come on out," he said impatiently. A haunting sound made him look around. The dark trees were swaying slowly. A quick shadow lifted into the sky. *Just a bird,* Timo thought, relieved, but his muscles stayed tense.

The window closed soundlessly. Timo waited quietly, rubbing his cold feet across the ground. After a few minutes the back door of Dino's house opened with an annoying squeal. Dino appeared dressed in dark green pants, a brown sweater and a dark cloak. Now Timo regretted he hadn't brought his cloak. He had chosen to wear his school uniform made out of a special, thin fabric that fitted like a second skin. It showed the school's colors, blue and yellow. Timo knew that the long, strong claws of the cold downdraft would not be able to pierce this special fabric. Though shivering, he smiled with relief when he saw his friend. He knew this day would bring his great success.

"Follow me," Timo whispered. He ran up the small slope and through the adjacent forest. Adrenaline rushed through his body and he ran as fast as possible.

"Wait," an exhausted voice yelled after him.

Timo stopped to wait under an old oak tree in which a large grey owl that had just returned from its nightly hunt was sitting on a large branch. The owl watched as an exhausted Dino reached the tree. After Dino was able to catch his breath and the two boys continued to run to the Cliff, the owl jumped from its branch, opened its grey wings and flew into the dark sky following the two boys from a safe distance.

"Hush," Dino cautioned the owl and tried to scare it away. He picked up a stone from the ground and was about to throw it at the night hunter when Timo stopped him.

"No," Timo said. "Owls bring luck."

As if the owl had understood Timo's words, it answered, "Hoot, Hoot, Hoot."

"Are you superstitious?" Dino asked. The owl's cry irritated him.

"No, but I have heard the old stories about the friendship between the owls and our people," Timo explained. Dino also knew those stories. His grandfather had told him of how life used to be for his people.

"You mean the story that owls are part of the spirit world and have the Spirit Knowledge?"

"Yes," Timo replied, "and how owls help carry the souls of the dead into the afterworld."

Dino watched the owl for a moment then looked down at the rock in his hand. Ashamed, he dropped it.

The sun was just above the top of the trees in the east by the time the boys reached the edge of the Cliff. "I hate this place," Dino said suddenly. "It is here they execute that stupid law."

"It is here the Rescue Flyers have to prove themselves," Timo replied. He knew the law Dino was talking about and a cold, uneasy feeling crept through his bones. Looking into the distance, he tried to think about something different. "What a view!" Timo said jubilantly and in a slightly exaggerated way to overcome his own fear. "Look, down there - the Flatlands. I would love to walk through the green forests and run across the yellow steppe. Look at the great lake! It is so blue and inviting. I would love to swim in it. Did you know there is a Wanderer village on the other side of the lake? Do you think they watch the mountains and talk about us, the Flyers?"

"They do for sure. They are afraid of us, and they hate us," Dino said.

"I hate them too, and you know why." After a long silence Timo continued. "Do you think there might be a beautiful girl down there who would like to meet a brave Flyer?"

"You are such a romantic, Timo," Dino joked.

"Why do you say that?"

"Look at you, just finished grade eight and you want to jump off the Cliff and meet beautiful Wanderer girls. In grade four you jumped from the top of the tallest tree at school and broke your arm. In grade six you were almost eaten alive when you walked into Wolf Forest to watch the young wolf puppies play. I still wonder how you escaped. In grade seven you played air ball with the big guys from grade ten and got a bloodied nose and dislocated shoulder. Everyone knows your name because of your stunts."

"They are not stunts," Timo said angrily, but he was angry and sad at the same time. "I just want to be . . . ," he started, but didn't finish. He lowered his head slowly and memories of his father drifted by in his mind.

The two boys stood quietly side by side for a while appreciating the silence between them and admiring the landscape that opened up below them. Timo's father had been killed somewhere down there in the distance. Timo didn't know exactly where, but he remembered the morning his mother had entered his room, her eyes red from crying. He hadn't cried. He'd felt that not crying was a way to show he could be strong, but he remembered the feeling of sadness and loneliness that had filled his heart at that moment. The Wanderers, those savages occupying the flatlands and grasslands below, had killed his father, and one day Timo would be strong enough to avenge his father's death.

"How strong is the updraft?" Timo suddenly asked, breaking the silence.

"I don't know," Dino answered, surprised as if waking from a lovely dream, "but look at the shape of the cumulus clouds and the mist lingering above the lake. See those individual tower clouds? They could quite quickly become cumulonimbus clouds that bring thunderstorms, and you know what that means!"

"No, I don't," Timo said. "That's grade nine stuff."

"It means a gust front can form, building a boundary that separates a cold downdraft from the warm, humid surface air that forms an updraft."

"So, what are you saying?"

"Instead of the updraft you need to survive your jump, you might be confronted with a cold downdraft that will kill you."

"How do you know all this stuff?"

"I like books, and I like to read ahead. Today is not a good day for your jump. Let's go back and try tomorrow."

"No, Dino," Timo almost yelled. "Today is a good day, as good as any other. You are here to tell me when the time is right to jump," Timo demanded. He opened his wings and moved them up and down, stretching them to get ready. Suddenly, a cold breeze touched his face, almost gently. He was surprised to feel a sharp pain, like a cold knife slicing through his warm skin. Dino had just explained what that might mean: the downdraft, almost certain death. He looked at his friend, concerned that Dino might have noticed the cold as well. Luckily Dino had been busy taking his notes out of his backpack and was now studying them.

"The sun has to climb some more," Dino said nervously. "She has to touch the tip of that tree over there, and the tree's shadow has to touch the stone over there. Then the updraft should be strong enough. I did the calculations as they have taught us at school." He looked up to smile proudly at Timo.

Timo had already walked to the edge of the Cliff; his bare toes were hanging over the rocks. He had to believe Dino was wrong. He felt the cold touch of the deadly downdraft again, but he couldn't back away. He had to do this today. He had dreamt of it and of the owl. He looked straight down The Cliff at the endless abyss of sharp rocks jutting from the mountain face; doubt crept into his mind.

"Not yet!" Dino yelled.

"I know, I know," Timo hissed angrily through clenched teeth. His father had been a Rescue Flyer, and the Rescue Flyers were the best-trained Flyers of them all. There were also Storm Flyers, trained to fly during the strongest winds and thunderstorms in the fall and spring; Rain Flyers, trained to fly during snowstorms and heavy rainfalls in the winter months; and War Flyers, trained to fight the Wanderers if they came too close to the mountains. But the Rescue Flyers were trained to fly anytime, anywhere, and under any weather conditions. His father had been the best Rescue Flyer ever.

The cold breeze touched him again. *Downdraft*, his mind screamed.

A few mountain birds were flying high in the sky and their songs reached Timo's ears. He smiled sadly. He, too, knew how to fly high in the blue sky. Actually, he was the best and fastest Flyer of his class, even of the class one year ahead of him. Everyone looked up to him and admired him for his talent, though when it came to math and writing, he was an average student. Flying was what he loved; he did it instinctively and by listening to his senses, by smelling the wind and feeling the air, not by mathematical formulas.

"Everyone has a talent," he used to say. "Mine is neither math nor writing."

The young girls in his school loved him. He had inherited soft, green eyes from his mother and strong high cheekbones from his father. He walked with his head held high; his long, brown hair swung gently across his shoulders. Deep down, however, he felt unsure about himself. He felt weaker than he appeared, and he was disillusioned about his ability. He believed he had to prove he was as strong and as talented as his father.

The cold breeze touched him again. He took a deep breath, inhaling the cold, for he also felt the warm air slowly rising from the mountainside.

It will be fine, he thought, a bit desperately. *The air smells right.*

"A few more minutes," called his friend. Dino's voice sounded muffled, as if filtered through a dense, impenetrable fog. Timo looked down the Cliff again. It looked steeper and deeper than before. He had stood here many times, unnoticed by those with an interest in seeing him here for the final testing of trained Rescue Flyers. Like the other times he had stood here, he imagined his father's face and his father's blue eyes smiling at him. He missed his father so much.

Suddenly he felt the sun on his face as it rose over the mountain peak. The warm rays tingled his nose and made him want to sneeze.

It will be fine, he told himself again. *The warm updraft will come.*

"The tree's shadow is creeping closer to the stone," Dino yelled in the background. Even he was excited now and had forgotten to worry. "I will start to count down from ten." Timo turned his head to see his friend standing over the tree's shadow; Dino was watching closely.

"Get ready, Timo!" Dino's voice echoed along the Cliff. "Here we go. Ten, nine . . . ."

Timo again looked down towards the Flatlands and the great, blue lake. For a split second he thought of the Wanderers living there. *Why would they have killed my father?* He wondered, but quickly focused on his challenge again. He spread his wings wide and moved them up and down. Though his wing muscles felt tense, he was strong and determined. He could feel every feather and every blood vessel.

"Eight, seven . . . ."

Timo smelled the air again; he closed his wings and folded them so they were close to his body as he had seen the Rescue Flyers do before they jumped off the Cliff.

"Six, five . . . ."

After I jump I have to count to seven before opening my wings, just like the Rescue Flyers do when they take their final test before being accepted into the Hall of Glory.

"Four, three . . . ."

He was deep in thought now, smelling and feeling, but no longer listening to his friend's countdown. In his mind he was already racing down the Cliff. Suddenly he heard, "Go!" Dino's shout made him jump head first down the Cliff into the abyss below.

Timo felt his feet leave the top of the Cliff. The wind rushed through his hair with ever-increasing force and speed. His heart pounded loudly, pumping his bubbling blood through his pulsating veins. Every other young Flyer would have panicked by now, but Timo felt wonderful; he was in his element. Weightlessness and the endless freedom of flying that was what he lived for. Today he would prove he was worthy of his father's pride.

There it was again; he sensed it very clearly now, the cold breeze. This time it was surrounding him, clinging to him, grabbing him like the claws of the large golden eagle that soared high in the sky above the Mountain of Sun. Timo's eyes widened.

"Seven!" he shouted and tried to open his wings, but he couldn't! The cold breeze had taken hold of his body and wouldn't release it. His school uniform didn't help. The ground quickly came closer and closer. He tried to open his wings again and again and again, but failed each time. He remembered his fall from the tall tree and the pain he had felt when his arm had broken, but remained calm. He didn't panic. He didn't scream. He knew the updraft would come; he only hoped it would come soon.

Dino was kneeling at the edge of the Cliff when he saw his friend disappear in the distance. He had watched Timo's body shrink to a small point.

"Open your wings!" he yelled. "Why don't you open your wings?"

"Wings!" Timo heard the echo coming from another mountain. The wind hissed in his ears and he began to tumble, like someone caught in a huge wave. Over and over he was tossed in a stream of air. There was no way of telling which way was up and which way was down. He forced his arms and legs outward to form an X. The tumbling slowly stopped but he continued to race toward the ground, head first. He concentrated and focused on what his senses and instincts were telling him. He felt the air temperature, the wind speed, the humidity. He observed the tower clouds in the sky and he suddenly knew what to do. By slightly moving his arms and legs in opposite directions he altered his position. He was no

9

longer racing down headfirst but moving sideways, parallel to the ground. He tried to open his wings again and they moved a little. Ever so slowly they opened. His wing muscles were too tight. To give them the strength he needed he pushed blood into them until it hurt.

"Don't give up," he yelled to himself. "You can do it." With a sudden rush, the cold let go of him and his wings opened completely. Pain charged through his back, unimaginable pain. The oncoming wind tried to bend his wings back, almost ripping them out. Timo screamed and tears filled his eyes. His tears were immediately grabbed by the wind and dispersed into the air. His vision blurred, but he held on. Then he felt it, the warm updraft. He was pushed up and his fall stopped. For a second he was gliding a few meters above the ground, then suddenly his strained wing muscles gave way and he crashed into the grass.

Everything around him was dark and he wasn't able to move. Timo felt as if all the bones in his body were broken; it hurt to breathe. Lying on his belly, he felt around carefully. His hands touched soft moss. *No rocks*, he thought with relief.

"I am still alive," he whispered.

"Yes, barely," a deep voice answered. "You were lucky."

Timo slowly tried to open his eyes, but his eyelashes were covered with blood. A cold, wet cloth landed on top of his hand.

"Wipe the blood off your face and sit up," the voice commanded. "What were you thinking, jumping off the Cliff?" the voice boomed.

"I can't move," Timo said. He was not worried about the consequences of being discovered; he was proud of what he had done.

"You try to be the big Flyer, risking your life, and now you can't even get up? Try again," the voice commanded, even angrier than before.

Timo slowly moved to his knees. It felt like many minutes before he was able to turn around and face the voice. He wiped his face and opened his eyes. The rising sun blinded him and his head pounded with pain. *It is not midday yet,* he thought. *I wonder how long I've been lying here.*

Something moved between him and the blinding sun. Timo was suddenly looking into a pair of blue, sparkling but angry eyes. A tall, muscular Flyer was standing in front of him.

"Aldor," Timo whispered respectfully.

"I was about to rescue you when the updraft came and stopped your fall. It can't really be called a flight. What a ridiculous idea to jump off the Cliff! What were you thinking? You are gifted and intelligent. Why this stupid stunt?"

"How did you know?"

"I have been watching you for a while now, since your jump from the tree. You have the gift of the ancient Flyers. Only a few have it. Your father had it. I have it. You can sense the wind and smell the air. You can feel the drafts and taste the humidity. Right?"

"Yes."

"So tell me, why did you jump before you're ready? You are impatient, and impatience can be deadly! You must control it. Now tell me." Aldor's voice echoed in Timo's head and he sensed how angry the experienced Flyer was.

Aldor was Lord of the Rescue Flyers and thus a member of the Council that met regularly on top of the Mountain of Clouds. The Council discussed and decided all issues that affected all Flyers and the mountains. Timo briefly looked at Aldor; he admired him tremendously, as did all the boys in his school. Many stories were told about Aldor's strength and

11

heroism, about his wisdom and knowledge, about his fairness and kindness. Timo had never seen him so angry. A tight wrinkle creased Aldor's forehead and his eyes looked stern and disappointed with Timo.

"I don't know," Timo finally answered, lowering his eyes.

"Don't know? You can do better than that. Tell me!" Aldor demanded.

"I just wanted to be . . . ," he stammered but didn't finish. He lowered his head and looked at the soft green grass in front of him. There was a slight dent in the ground where he had landed.

Timo turned around and, filled with anguish, suddenly cried out, "I just wanted to be like my father!" His eyes were full of tears that made his surroundings foggy again. He didn't know if his tears came from anger or from frustration, but suspected it was probably both, plus the emotional and physical pain he felt.

Aldor stepped closer and put his hand on Timo's shoulder. "I know," Aldor said softly. "I miss him too, very much. He was my best friend and my closest confidant. I shared everything with him and he with me. We were comrades in war, but I couldn't save him." He paused for a moment, thinking about his friend, trying to visualize his face. "Come on," Aldor said. "Let me take you to the Mountain of Life to get you fixed up. I think you need at least seven stitches to close the cut above your left eye. You know about the consequences of your foolish act, I presume?"

Timo quietly nodded.

"Good. I will talk to the Council and see what I can do on your behalf, but I don't promise anything. You might lose your privilege to fly for at least a year, plus some other punishment."

Timo was angry, his hands clenched in fists, but he didn't complain to Aldor. Losing the right to fly for a year was the worst punishment for anyone who loved and lived for flying. It was almost as bad as losing one's legs. Although Timo had known beforehand about the consequences, he was proud of his accomplishment and ready to defend his actions. "But I was flying, and I proved that I am ready to take the final test to become a Rescue Flyer," Timo protested.

"You call this flying? Your landing was more like a lucky crash. If you are ready to become a Rescue Flyer, how do you explain the cut above your eye?" Aldor was smiling. His anger was gone, but his concern for Timo's future was stronger than ever. He understood that Timo was longing for his father and looking for his approval, but how could one get approval from a dead Flyer?

Timo slowly straightened, despite his pain, and looked into Aldor's eyes. "Thank you," he said. Everything around him became dark and he started to sink to the ground.

Aldor carefully lifted Timo into his arms and jumped into the air. He moved his large wings up and down. The two Flyers rose slowly and with the help of the updraft were lifted higher and higher into the blue sky.

Dino saw the muscular Rescue Flyer with Timo's lifeless body in his arms rising from the abyss. "Oh no," he cried. "Timo."

He watched as Aldor turned west and flew towards the Mountain of Life. He knew where Aldor was taking Timo. He quickly collected his drawings and sketches and walked home slowly. He was scared and worried. He knew about the punishment that would come, but he didn't care, as long as Timo survived.

"It is my fault," Dino confessed to the trees that lined the path home. "I should have stopped him."

CHAPTER TWO

The Mountain of Life

Aldor soared gracefully towards the group of mountains that stood in the North. He was holding Timo carefully in his arms, protecting him like a younger child though he was already fourteen years old.

"I love our mountains," declared Aldor. He continued to watch the area below him while flying closer to the clouds.

Timo looked around just a little while fading in and out of consciousness. He felt as though he were flying by himself, the cold air rushing through the feathers of his wide open wings. He flew over the tallest mountain where the golden eagle lived and which was named the Mountain of Clouds because its peak remained hidden behind the clouds. He remembered the large meeting hall built out of old, weathered rock. It stood lonely on the mountaintop and was where the Council met. *It is where your punishment awaits you*, he thought.

He opened his eyes briefly to see in the distance the Mountain of Sun where it was always bright and warm. One day he would go there to train with the Rescue Flyers. Their training ground was built on the plateau above the tree line.

Timo closed his eyes again. He knew the mountains by heart. He loved them and had explored them diligently, even though he did not have permission to venture freely into all the places he had visited. The Mountain of Glory, where the old stone library stood, was off limits to the younger Flyers, but he had been there anyway. He had sneaked through the hallways and had admired the many ancient books that held the history of the Flyers. He had marveled over the engravings on the library walls that listed all the names of the Rescue Flyers.

When he had been caught by one of the Elders who lived there, instead of punishing him, the wise and knowledgeable old Flyer had shown him around the old hallways. The Elder had been happy to see a young Flyer interested in history and the ways of his ancestors. Timo had felt peaceful among the old books and their wisdom, almost as peaceful as he felt now in the arms of Aldor.

"The Mountain of Life," Aldor announced suddenly, and Timo opened his eyes, startled by the roaring voice. Right in front of them arose a small mountain. The healers lived there in the Great Halls of Vita. New life was born and the injured treated there. The sick visited the halls and returned home healthy. Eventually all Flyers entered the Halls of Healing, just before their great journey to the afterworld.

"Where are we?" Timo whispered, looking around anxiously. The initial pain that had started in his chest began to radiate through his whole body. His face was contorted with pain.

Aldor soared carefully in a large circle, slowing his flight. "Almost there," Aldor replied reassuringly. The pain in Timo's voice concerned him. His approach to the Mountain of Life was swift, but controlled and careful. He flew towards the large plateau that was part of the entrance to the Halls of Healing. A mile to the left of the wooden building a small waterfall rushed down from the next highest plateau and filled a small lake. The air was fresh and, when the wind blew from the West, the mist from the waterfall was caught in the branches of the birch trees surrounding the plateau.

The landing was soft. Timo was conscious but felt dizzy and disoriented. Aldor gently lowered him to the ground. With a slight, painful breath, Timo tried to stand but quickly collapsed. Aldor caught him just before he hit the ground.

"Are you all right?" Aldor asked, concerned.

15

"No," Timo whispered painfully, close to losing consciousness again. He thought about his home on the Mountain of Wind, the mountain where most of the Flyers lived with their families. It was the largest mountain with a vast plateau that stretched for miles and miles, with beautiful valleys, rich cornfields, small, comfortable villages, old forests, and refreshing waterfalls; a place of beauty and splendor. He thought about his school and the large meadow where all the celebrations took place.

Will I ever see my home again? He wondered. Timo lifted his head and saw the dark spot high up in the Mountain of Clouds. *The War Flyers' fortress.* A feeling of mistrust and anger rose up in Timo. "Mountain of the War Flyers," he snarled.

"What did you say, Timo?" Aldor asked, looking at the young Flyer.

"Nothing," Timo said dryly.

"Hang in there!" Aldor encouraged.

Aldor pushed open the large, wooden doors that led into the Halls of Healing and walked in. Timo felt every one of Aldor's steps painfully vibrating through his own body. He tried to lift his arm, but his pain-ridden body didn't listen to his commands.

"Over there." Aldor pointed towards the end of the hall. "The Healing Flyer."

Aldor walked toward a tall, elderly, grey-haired Flyer. Against the wall stood a freshly made bed where Aldor laid Timo. Timo almost screamed from the pain; each breath he took hurt, and the light in the room was so bright his eyes began to ache. He didn't notice the enchanted carvings in the wooden walls and columns that surrounded him. They showed scenes of childbirth, of golden sunrays, of the five mountains, and of the doorway that led into the afterworld, the doorway

Timo's father had walked through four years ago. Scenes of giving life and taking life, fighting and war, and scenes of the Wanderers and Flyers living together peacefully were engraved in the dark brown wood. His pain distracted him from these scenes; he was unable to appreciate the important history these carvings represented.

The Healing Flyer greeted Aldor like an old friend. They talked briefly to one another and looked at Timo, who didn't hear any of their conversation. He was tired and ready to go to sleep. Suddenly, he was lifted up and carried carefully to an examination table. A large oval light shone in his eyes, forcing him to close them. Hands touched and felt him all over. He groaned and sometimes screamed in pain. As suddenly as it had started, it stopped. He carefully opened his eyes; the bright light was still there, so when he saw a long, curved needle coming close to his left eye he started to pass out. Before he blacked out completely, he heard the Healing Flyer say to Aldor, "Nothing is broken, but everything is bruised. His arms, his legs, his ribs, his knees, and worst of all, his wing muscles have been stretched to their limit. He will be in a lot of pain for at least a week. We will keep him here for observation for a few days." Then darkness and silence overwhelmed him.

*** *** ***

The wind was playing with the branches and leaves of the trees that surrounded the Halls of Healing. It howled and whistled and whooshed; Timo listened to the song the wind was singing for him. He loved this wild song of freedom and ferocity. Nothing made him happier than the wind in his face and the air in his wings. When he finally opened his eyes he found himself lying in a soft bed of white linen. The room he was in was larger than his bedroom at home, but there was hardly any furniture. The walls were bone white. In one corner stood a small white desk, beside it stood a brown, wooden chair. The sign above his bed read, "What goes up must come down." A small child must have made it since the handwriting was uneven. Timo smiled. *This is so true*, he thought, barely remembering what had happened the previous afternoon. He looked out the big window in his room to watch the endless fall of water rushing down the cliff. His smile was replaced by a painful grimace when he tried to inhale deeply. *The Cliff*, he suddenly remembered as the pain rushed through his body. He realized what had happened and now remembered it vividly.

"I did it," he whispered. Again he tried to take a deep breath and started to cough. A sharp pain filled his lungs and chest. His bruised ribs and the inflamed muscles around them felt like they would burst. Tears ran down his face and he held his chest with his hands, worried that it might break apart.

"Good morning," Aldor said as he entered the room. "I see you are paying for yesterday's folly. Six stitches, the scar above your left eye will forever remind you of it." A smile started to form around Aldor's lips, but he quickly became serious again.

"I saw your mother yesterday, after I left you. She was very upset, but relieved when I told her you will be fine. She wanted to come immediately, but I stopped her. I told her you will need lots of rest and that I will look after you for a while. She was insistent and almost pushed me out of her way. You have a strong, resolute mother. I hope stopping her was in your interest?" Aldor looked sternly at Timo.

"Yes," whispered Timo, his chest still burning from the coughing. He admired his mother and loved her dearly but was grateful for Aldor's consideration. "Thank you for stopping her. I would not have heard the end of it."

"You will still have to face her, and she will not be easy with you. You are definitely grounded and then some. She will visit you in a few days. Now, to a more serious matter. I also met with the Council last night. Most of the members were upset and angry. The Golden Eagle had told them about your foolishness. The mountain birds had seen you and reported the events to him. I was able to calm them down. They want to meet you and talk with you to give you a chance to explain yourself. Wardor is especially interested in your story."

"Wardor," Timo groaned. "Lord of the War Flyers? Why him? Everyone is afraid of him."

"Yes, he is quite fearsome. I think he wants to set an example, to show he doesn't tolerate your behavior. He knows you have the gift, which he himself does not have. He is jealous of you, as he was jealous of your father and is jealous of me."

"What about Dino?" asked Timo.

"Your concern for your friend shows loyalty and commitment. Good for you," Aldor said, pleased with Timo. "He is fine. He was very worried and concerned about you, too. He really likes you. He is a good friend. He has nothing to worry about from the Council, I made sure of that, but his parents are a different story. They've grounded him for a month. I talked to him after the grounding and he seems fine with it. He is into books and science and math. As long as he has his books he will be okay."

Timo smiled. "Yes, that is my friend Dino. His nose is always in books. He knows a lot about clouds and winds, temperatures and humidity. He is not into flying, not like me. I love to fly. I have to open my wings and feel the wind playing with them. I have to feel the wind in my face." Timo suddenly looked concerned. "Will they take that away from me?" he asked.

"It is possible, if Wardor has his way. We must wait and see. Before they decide on the penalty for your actions, they will listen to you. Come to your hearing prepared and be ready to answer some tough questions. You have been given three days to recover. You are expected to appear in front of the Council on the evening of the third day, just before the sun disappears behind the trees. You must come alone to the Mountain of Clouds."

"Only three days?"

"Yes. Will you be able to fly by then?"

"I will try."

"Trying will not be enough. No one is permitted to help you get to the mountain. You must depend on your strength alone. If you don't appear on time, you will automatically receive the maximum penalty." Aldor looked directly into Timo's eyes before continuing. "No more flying at all. Right now, if you show up, I think you might get one year of no flying and an additional year in the service of the Council, which also means no flying."

"Two years without flying?" Timo was horrified. "I will not survive that!" he exclaimed.

"Yes, you will," Aldor said calmly. "If you really want to do it, with all your heart and with all your will, I will be on your side as a guardian defender. We will face the accusations and threats of Wardor together."

"I will come. I will be ready, no matter how much pain it involves. Thank you, Aldor." Bravely Timo tried to sit up in his bed, but his muscles didn't listen to him. They only caused him pain. "Why do you do this?" Timo asked, his eyes filling with tears from the pain.

"Your father was my friend. As his friend it is my duty to help and protect you. I don't want to replace him and I can't, but allow me to guide you where and whenever possible."

"How did he die?" Timo suddenly asked. He had never asked this question before. His mother had told him about the ambush and how the Wanderers had been involved, but he longed to find out specifically what had happened to his father. He hadn't wanted to burden his mother, and he had no one else to ask.

"You need your rest now," Aldor cautioned. "A Healing Flyer will come soon and work with you to get your muscles moving again. Your rehabilitation will be painful, very painful. Believe me, I know." After seeing Timo's sad eyes he added, "I am not trying to get out of giving you an answer. I was there when your father died. I will tell you the truth, I promise, but this is neither the time nor the place." He held out his hand to Timo and Timo took it. A warm flow of energy flew between the two Flyers; their gift united them.

"I promise you, between two Rescue Flyers. Honor and loyalty is our guidance, and you have both," Aldor proclaimed before he let go of Timo's hand, then he turned around and walked out of the room.

Timo was alone again. The meeting with Aldor and the words he had spoken overwhelmed him. "Honor and loyalty," he repeated to himself. "Thank you, Aldor, for your trust. I promise I will not disappoint you," he whispered.

*** *** ***

Timo closed his eyes. The wind was still singing its song. It called for him and he desired to be outside with open wings. Timo traveled mentally through his body, focusing on every muscle and bone. He could feel them all and tried to speak with them, but all he heard were their painful cries.

I will be ready for the Council, he insisted. *I must be ready for the Council*, he pleaded.

A soft knock at the door brought him back to the present. "Yes," Timo said and opened his eyes. He saw a beautiful

Healing Flyer standing in his room. Black, curly hair framed her brown, smooth face. Her dark eyes twinkled and looked at him intently. He swallowed nervously.

"Are you Timo?" she asked. Her voice sounded like the rushing of the wind that passed by his ears on a warm summer evening flight. He no longer heard the song of the wind that had tempted him before.

"Yes," he rasped skittishly.

"My name is Rare. I will be helping you gain control over your muscles again. Don't worry, I will be careful." Rare walked briskly towards his bed, removed the blanket that was keeping Timo warm and began to work on his legs. She moved his feet, bent his knees, and twisted his hips.

"Everything seems to be fine with your legs," she explained.

Then Rare took his arms and bent his wrists and fingers, twisted his elbows and stretched his shoulders. "Everything seems to be fine here, too."

However, when Rare touched his ribs and his wings, Timo thought he was going to faint. He didn't scream, but he couldn't stop groaning. "Well," Rare said seriously. "I guess I've found the problem areas. We will start with small exercises and stretching. Stretching is most important, and your breathing deeply will likely be the fastest way to ease the pain in your chest and ribs."

The exercises Rare continued with became increasingly painful. Although Timo didn't want to cry, he could not control the tears running down his cheeks, and he almost fainted a couple of times from the pain. *Smart*, he thought. *They've sent a beautiful Healing Flyer so I won't act and scream like a baby.*

However, eventually he couldn't help screaming, and at the end of the day he lay in his bed exhausted, with red eyes and injured pride. Never in his life had he experienced so much pain, not even during or right after his failed landing at the bottom of the Cliff. At the same time, Rare's work had had a miraculous effect on his body. His muscles were beginning to listen to him again, and he was able to get into and out of bed without any help. When he thought about Rare returning the next morning his body twitched slightly. Nonetheless, he looked forward to seeing her again, despite all the pain that came with her arrival.

*** *** ***

The night came quickly to the Mountain of Life and the lights in the great hallways were dimmed. A bright full moon shone through Timo's window, watching him sleep peacefully. When he first woke up he didn't know where he was or what time it was. He looked out the window to see two small shadows flying in front of the moon. He wondered about this for only a second, and then quickly fell asleep again.

Not long after, a sadly familiar sound woke him up. Someone was crying. Timo remembered the long nights he'd lain awake in his bedroom listening to his mother crying after his father's death. He'd felt for her so deeply because he'd felt the same loneliness and sadness. He'd often gone to her in her room to sit beside her on her bed until she had cried herself to sleep. One morning, though, she had come out of her bedroom with a smile on her face. "We will be fine," she had said and had given Timo a long, loving hug.

Timo turned slowly and got out of bed. He walked stiffly to the door and looked into the hallway. A young female Flyer was sitting in one of the corners opposite his room; her back was against the wall and her knees pulled up under her chin.

"Val," he whispered, "is that you?" He recognized the long, blonde hair shining in the white light of the moon. She was the only Flyer he knew who had that kind of hair; all the other girls' hair was dark, even black.

Val was in his class and he was somewhat fond of her, not only because she was an excellent Flyer. She lived with her family on the other side of his small village. He would run into her from time to time in the Market Square or on the way to school. He always wanted to talk to her, to get to know her better, but each time he readied himself to approach her, his voice gave way and he simply waved hello.

"Timo?" she answered in disbelief. "What are you doing here?"

"Oh, just a little accident," he answered hesitantly.

"Another stunt?"

"Why does everyone think I am doing stunts?" he protested.

"Sorry," Val whispered, wiping the tears from her cheeks.

"No," Timo replied. "I am sorry. You are right. My actions speak for themselves, I guess. So why are you crying?" He had moved closer to her and was now sitting beside her. The hallway was empty and the wooden floor where they sat was cold. Val was leaning against the wall beside a large potted green tree, its branches spreading above her head as if trying to protect her from some invisible harm. The moonlight played softly with her blonde hair and sparkled in her green eyes.

"We were expecting a baby, actually my mother was expecting," she corrected herself. Timo looked at her; he tried to say something but couldn't find the words. "Everything went fine. The last nine months were a wonderful experience for us — no morning sickness, hardly any pain, and my mother could feel the baby moving around a lot in the last few weeks. The birth went well, too. The contractions started this morning as the sun rose in the east. The baby took his first breath just three hours ago. I heard him cry a strong, healthy cry, loud and hearty. Two Healing Flyers took him away, for examination they had said, but when they returned they reported that the baby had died." Tears rolled down her cheeks again.

"How is that possible?" Timo asked.

"They said the baby's heart failed, even though they tried everything in their power to rescue him. I don't believe them. Something isn't right."

"What do you mean?"

"When I walked around the Halls of Healing to find a quiet place to be alone, I heard a baby cry very close to here, but my mother has been the only Flyer here today to give birth."

"Maybe it was another baby from a previous day?"

"No," Val insisted. "I recognized his cry. I'm sure it was him. You know," she said hesitantly," I can hear the wind sing and I can remember every note of every song." She paused to look at Timo. She waited for his response, but Timo just looked encouragingly into her eyes. He knew the songs she was talking about.

"The wind sings different songs, depending on the time of day, on the temperature, on the season. I can hear them and understand them," she said. Timo listened intently and smiled because he knew what Val was talking about, but Val took the smile the wrong way.

"You don't understand. Please don't laugh," she said quickly.

"I do understand," Timo responded, "and I'm not laughing."

"I haven't told anyone about these songs I hear, not even my parents or my best friend. They wouldn't understand. I don't know why I'm telling you." She paused for only a moment, then said with determination in her voice and a flicker

25

in her eye, "My brother is still alive. I heard him cry. Something wicked is happening here." She found comfort in Timo's quiet listening. She didn't want to hear any comments or stupid questions; she just needed someone who would listen without responding. "I also saw two Healing Flyers leaving the Mountain of Life a while ago," she continued. "They were flying toward the Mountain of Glory and one of them was carrying a small bundle wrapped in a white blanket."

"I saw two shadows in front of the moon when I woke up," Timo replied. "I thought I was still dreaming. To the Mountain of Glory, the home of the Elders?" Timo added. "What would they be doing there in the middle of the night?"

"You saw them too!" Val cried. She searched Timo's eyes hopefully. "I don't know what is happening, but that little bundle was moving and crying. I also saw a faint light being lit on top of the Mountain of Glory." Suddenly, Val sat perfectly still, then placed one finger on her lip and listened into the darkness. "Footsteps. I have to go." Val was up and gone in a second, quietly, like a shadow.

It took Timo a while to get up; his muscles were no longer listening to him. The crouched position and the cold floor he had been sitting on made him feel numb. Small pearls of sweat formed on his forehead and he was breathing heavily by the time he finally reached his bed. He could hear the footsteps coming closer, their pounding echoing in the hallway. Luckily, they passed by his door and slowly faded away. Timo lay awake for a while and thought about Val.

"She has the gift," he thought. "She hears the wind like I do." He felt happy inside, not really knowing why. "I wonder what happened to her baby brother. What if she is right? Why would the Healing Flyers do such a thing?"

Eventually he was too tired to think, and he fell asleep. The moon passed through the sky and disappeared behind the mountains in the west.

Val, however, was wide-awake and focused, flying carefully through the moist air. Without making a sound, she glided toward the Mountain of Glory.

*** *** ***

Before the sun's rays illuminated the treetops of the Mountain of Life, Timo was rudely awakened by a cheerful voice.

"Get up, young Flyer. Another wonderful, fresh day for healing." Timo grimaced when he saw Rare standing beside his bed, even before they had started with the exercises. To his surprise, the morning began better than he had thought it would. Rare started with a gentle massage of his back muscles and upper shoulders. She carefully supported his wings and slowly opened them.

"Stand up, young Flyer," she encouraged, her breath tickling Timo's ears. He slowly moved out of his bed and stood on weak legs. They felt wobbly like after a long run, and he was afraid his calf muscles would cramp up, but Rare supported him. "Slowly now," she said. "Try to move your wings. I will help you." Timo concentrated; he could feel his wing muscles stretch as Rare slowly opened and closed his wings. "Now you try it on your own."

A sharp pain went through his muscles when Rare let go of his wings, but he was able to keep them open. "Very good," Rare said encouragingly. "Now slowly close them."

Sweat formed on Timo's forehead and upper lip, but ever so slowly his wings closed. "Excellent. Now open them!"

Timo groaned, then focused his energy and slowly opened his wings.

"Good. Now move them up and down."

Timo shook his head. "I can't."

"Yes, you can. Nothing is broken. Try it," Rare demanded.

His wings started to twitch, then slowly moved upward. The pain made him stop. "I can't!" Timo cried.

"Just do it. You can do it. You want to do it." The pleasantries in Rare's voice were gone. She wanted Timo to work harder, to work to the maximum of his ability. She pushed him as hard as she could. "Try harder!"

Timo was reminded of what Aldor had said. "Trying is not good enough, you have to do more." He was also reminded of the penalty he would receive if he did not succeed.

"I will fly," he hissed through clenched teeth, and his wings began to move slowly up and down, once, twice, three times, then he closed them again.

"Well done, Timo." Rare's friendly voice was back. "Now rest for a while and do the exercises again. The more often you do them, the sooner you will fly."

"Thank you, Rare," Timo whispered. He was exhausted and crawled back into his bed. Rare gave him another gentle massage then left him alone.

"I will fly again," Timo whispered to himself before he fell asleep.

The wind was singing a welcome lullaby when a soft knock on Timo's window woke him up. He held his breath and listened.

"Timo," whispered a familiar voice.

"Dino? What are you doing here? I thought you were grounded."

"I am, but I had to come. I sneaked away from school. I had to see you."

Timo slowly crawled out of bed and walked to the window. He pushed the glass panel aside and smiled at his worried friend. "This is so unlike you, you hate flying to other mountains. Thank you for coming."

"So how are you doing?" Dino replied. "When I saw the Flyer carrying you away I thought you were dead."

"I am fine," Timo lied. "No, that is not true. I am in a lot of pain and in two nights I have to face the Council."

"Can I help you?"

"Thank you, my friend, but I can't accept any help. I have to fly alone," Timo replied, then he quickly whispered, "Something is happening here. A baby went missing. Maybe you can keep your ears open and tell me if you hear anything unusual."

"What do you mean?"

"I can't explain, not now, but later. How are you doing?"

"I am grounded for sure. My parents were so mad I thought they would kill me. They yelled and screamed. I have to go now. School will start again soon. If I hear something, I will let you know. Take care, Timo."

"Take care, Dino. And thank you."

Dino walked away from the building, opened his wings and flew back to the Mountain of Wind, back to school. He had not seen the face peering through the window adjacent to Timo's room.

CHAPTER THREE

The Mountain of Glory

The night was black after the moon had vanished. No one saw Val flying away from the Mountain of Healing. Her spirits had lifted after she'd talked with Timo. She was surprised how mature he seemed to be, not like at school where he was always pretending to be in control. She liked Timo a lot.

Val was an outstanding student achieving straight A's in all her classes. All the students as well as her teachers liked her. She was responsible and always ready to help out when needed. To her, everybody was equal. For that both the talented and not so talented students respected her.

The cold air blew across Val's tanned face as she neared the home of the Elders. She had followed the light that shone from the top of the mountain. It shimmered through a colorful window in a large structure built of stone that looked like a castle from long ago with towers and lead glass windows. She had heard about the large library housed within the castle's walls, but she had never seen it. She knew this was the home of the Elders, the oldest and wisest Flyers.

She landed in front of the castle on a round plateau surrounded by a thick forest and thorny bushes. A small creek ran along the forest's edge until it tumbled down the cliff into the steep abyss below the Mountain of Glory. She moved closer to the window and saw two Healing Flyers walking along the long corridor. Proudly she thought *I can fly faster than any Healing Flyer.*

She quietly opened the old wooden doors and slipped quickly inside the library. The corridor walls were lined with shelves on which hundreds of thick books were neatly organized. In the blink of an eye she rushed down the hallway while the door closed quietly behind her. Hundreds of candles held by crystal holders snaked up the walls and brightened the otherwise dark hallways. In the distance she heard a choir singing a beautiful tune, but Val felt unwelcome here. She quickly followed the sound of retreating footsteps that led her deeper into the stone building. Suddenly, after taking a quick right turn, she stood in front of a massive, old wooden door. She carefully put her right ear to the cold surface. The singing had suddenly stopped. An ominous male voice was speaking on the other side of the door, but she couldn't understand what it said. A female voice responded. Val kneeled down and looked through the keyhole. The two Healing Flyers stood with their backs to the door. Six other Flyers, dressed in red robes, heads covered with yellow hoods, bent over a tiny bed. They were watching a small baby that lay calmly on white sheets.

"You are right," Val heard the male voice again. "No wings."

The baby moved and began to cry. "My brother," Val said, much louder than she'd intended. She had recognized his cry. One of the Healing Flyers turned around and looked at the door.

"Someone is at the door," the Flyer yelled. Val sprung up and ran back through the hallways. The door to the chamber opened briskly and slammed against the wall. The two Healing Flyers ran after Val.

Val wore a black coat, black pants, and black boots. Her blonde hair was bound in a ponytail and covered with a black hood. Like a shadow in the night she rushed through the library, feet hardly touching the ground. She reached the castle door before the Healing Flyers had turned the last corner. Val ran across the plateau and jumped over the small creek and thorny bushes. She crouched beside a small tree and waited.

She didn't want to fly. She watched as the two Flyers came running out of the old building, rushed across the plateau and jumped off the mountain. Soon they were soaring above the plateau, looking for her. After crisscrossing the plateau several times and circling in an ever-enlarging circle for twenty minutes, they returned. Before they disappeared into the stone building Val heard one of them say, "He has escaped. I hope it wasn't one of Wardor's spies."

Val was frightened and barely dared to breathe. She waited silently while dozens of thoughts ran through her head. *My brother is alive! Kidnapped! Why? In the realm of the Elders, kidnapped by Healing Flyers. What did they mean by 'No wings?'* Her head was spinning.

She waited another few minutes before coming out of her hiding spot. She stood behind some tall, thick bushes and listened carefully. When she didn't hear anything, she slid through the bushes, cautiously avoiding the long, pointy thorns, then jumped over the small creek and crouched down again. The moon had reappeared from behind the mountains in the north and was shining brightly. The castle's shadow darkened the other side of the plateau, but Val's side was as bright as day. When she was sure she didn't hear anything, she got up and started running toward the mountain's edge. Suddenly she noticed something moving in the sky. She dropped to the ground and hoped her black clothing would help her look like a rock. Two huge Flyers passed in front of the bright moon. Val saw bows and arrows in their hands and long swords strapped across their backs.

"War Flyers," she whispered. "Up here on the Mountain of Glory, in full armor. That is forbidden." She watched as they flew overhead. As soon as they were out of sight she got up and ran to the edge of the mountain. Without hesitating, she jumped off and opened her wings. The wind greeted her with a warm breeze.

"Welcome," it whispered into her ear. "You are not alone. Be careful, the War Flyers have spotted you."

"I hear you, Wind," Val replied. "Thank you."

Then another sound reached her sensitive ears, a hissing sound. Val ducked to her right, folded her wings and went into a nosedive. An arrow shot past her leg. A quick look behind confirmed the wind's warning: the two War Flyers were racing after her. *A Rescue Flyer is faster and quicker than a heavily armed War Flyer*, she thought nervously, trying to calm herself. Her special training on top of the Mountain of Sun had prepared her for situations like this. She continued her dive and the ground quickly came closer and closer. "Good," Val thought when the bright moon disappeared behind the mountains and the night grew dark again. The trees, bushes and landscape below had become a single grey patch.

Suddenly Val opened her wings and pulled to her left. A cold breeze touched her face and she knew she would soon be rid of her pursuers. *A cold breeze can be the best friend of a Rescue Flyer,* she thought. *It means a cold downdraft is near.*

Val knew that if a Flyer didn't know how to escape the deadly claws of a cold downdraft, that Flyer would fall to the ground like a heavy rock. She closed her wings again, but this time instead of going into a nosedive, she shot through the air in a horizontal line. Her legs were spread to form a V, which acted like the rudder of an old pirate ship, allowing her to steer safely through the cold claws waiting in front of her. Another quick move of her wings and she shot upwards, passing the War Flyers on their doomed way down. Val heard their screams as the claws of the cold downdraft grabbed them and they realized they were beyond the point of return. Two loud smashing sounds told her that the War Flyers had crashed; they would be following her no longer. Val was overcome with sorrow, afraid she might have killed two Flyers. She had never been in such a situation before; she had trained for escaping the cold downdraft, but not for escaping Flyers who tried to kill her.

Why would they want to kill me? Val wondered on her flight back to the Mountain of Life. *I have never heard of one Flyer killing another. What is happening?* She tried to put her mind at ease; she had acted in self-defense. She was certain the War Flyers would have killed her.

War Flyers in full armor, Elders and Healing Flyers at the same location examining a tiny baby late at night. It doesn't make any sense.

She was soaring now, high up in the sky. She saw the outline of the Halls of Healing and the faint landing light on the main plateau that was lit every night so those in need could find their way to a safe place.

If Timo hadn't been so impatient, he could have been with me on the Mountain of Sun and learned all that I have learned. Can I tell him what I have found out? Can I trust him? she wondered. *I have to tell someone, but not my mother. She wouldn't be able to handle it, not now. She is still too fragile after the bad news that her baby is dead. Not my father, he is too old fashioned and wouldn't understand. And Aldor is not close by. Timo has the gift. That almost makes him a Rescue Flyer. Aldor has told me that Timo has honor and loyalty.*

"I will have to trust him," she spoke in a whisper." He is the only one who will understand. I believe I can trust him," she stated firmly as she landed. Silently and quickly she moved through the dimly lit hallways and in no time stood at Timo's door. A loud snoring greeted her. *Tomorrow*, she thought, and quietly entered his room.

Standing by Timo's bed, she looked down at her friend sleeping calmly. *He looks very nice with his brown curly hair,* she thought, *and the cut above his eye will make him look somewhat distinguished one day.*

Suddenly, she heard footsteps approaching. She recognized them as the footsteps she had heard before. She left Timo's room in the nick of time.

*** *** ***

Before the sun touched the mountain peaks, Val was up again ready for another day, eager to tell Timo what had happened. She had spent the night in her mother's room. After dressing quietly, she bent down to give her sleeping mother a kiss. "Good morning," her mother said weakly. Val could hear the sadness and grief in her mother's voice.

"Good morning, mother. How are you?"

Her mother sat up, and Val saw the tears on her mother's face before her mother wiped them away with the back of her hand. She looked at her daughter. "We lost our baby," she cried. "I still hear him taking his first breath. What happened?"

Val returned to her mother's bed and sat down. She reached towards her and they held hands and comforted one another for a long time, until her mother stopped crying.

Val didn't know how to feel. She knew that her brother was still alive and she wanted to tell her mother this, but she also knew that her mother was fragile right now and it might be better to wait until Val understood better what was going on. "I am sorry," whispered Val.

"I know," her mother answered. "I didn't hear you come back last night. Where were you?"

"I was crying," Val answered quietly. "When I returned, you were already asleep and I didn't want to wake you."

"Thank you, my lovely daughter. Thank you for your help. I love you."

"I love you too, mother. Try to get some more rest. It is still early. I will be back later."

Val gave her mother a kiss on her right cheek and pulled the blanket up to cover her mother's shoulders. Then she turned around and walked out of the room. She felt the deep pain and emptiness of her mother, and while she walked through the Halls of Healing toward Timo's room, she promised, "I will find out what is happening to your son, mother, and I will bring him home."

When she approached Timo's room, she could hear wings flapping up and down slowly. "Good," Rare was saying. "Spread those wings of yours as far as you can. And if you keep exercising, by tomorrow, after our last session, you might be able to fly again. I hope so!"

Val sat down on the floor opposite Timo's room. She waited nervously and restlessly for Timo to finish his exercises. "Here," Rare continued. "Take this towel and wipe off those tears, and the sweat. Today was much better than yesterday. Your muscles are less cramped and more flexible. Don't you think so?"

Timo stood in front of his bed; sweat ran down his face and his T-shirt was soaked. "Yes," he hissed through clenched teeth. "Much better."

"See you tomorrow," Rare said as she left the room.

"Thank you," Timo responded. "Thank you for your help."

After hearing Rare reply in a friendly voice, "You are welcome!" Timo fell forward onto his bed with a relieved and exhausted sigh. He didn't hear Val enter his room. She was suddenly by his bed, touching him gently on the shoulder.

"I thought we were finished for today, Rare," he groaned.

"It's me, Val."

Timo turned around slowly and smiled. The morning sunlight illuminated Val's gentle face. Her blonde hair, still bound in a ponytail, shone brightly. She was very pretty; her green eyes looked intently at Timo.

"You scared me," was all he could say, immediately regretting it.

"I need your help, please," she said, ignoring his words.

"Yes, sure. What can I do?"

Val sat down beside him on the bed and told him all she had learned and witnessed the previous night. She whispered the whole story, looking up nervously each time she heard a noise.

"They said 'No wings.' What does that mean? Then the War Flyers chased me and tried to kill me," Val explained.

Timo listened attentively, asking the odd question to get some events explained in more detail. He shook his head several times in disbelief. "What is going on?" he asked.

"I don't know. It doesn't make sense, but I have more to tell you. You can't tell anyone about this or I will never speak to you again. I will curse you for the rest of your life."

Timo looked at her in a disappointed way. Her words stung like barbs, but he saw the sincerity in her face and he understood Val's concern. *She doesn't really know me*, he thought. *We are schoolmates, but she has to be careful, especially after what she saw last night.*

"Promise," he said. "Not a word, to anyone." He actually felt quite proud at that moment. Val was willing to confide in him.

"I am enrolled in a special program," Val started hesitantly, whispering again. "I have been selected to join the Rescue Flyer program on the Mountain of Sun. I have been there after school every day since the middle of the last school term."

Timo was shocked. "You were where?" He had always dreamed about joining that program. Every young Flyer had heard about it, and he knew that only a few were selected secretly every year. He had been waiting for his call ever since he could remember. A feeling of jealousy, disappointment and unhappiness came over him. *Why her?* He thought. *She is very good, but not as good as I am. Why her and not me?*

"I am sorry," Val said, noticing Timo's disappointment.

"Don't be," Timo said. "You deserve it. You have been working hard all year." He knew he shouldn't blame her for him not being selected. *It's my own fault. If I hadn't been so busy with proving something, I might have been selected as well. Aldor was right about the importance of patience.* Timo smiled at Val.

"Tell me about the Mountain of Sun," he said.

"It is a wonderful place. A Rescue Flyer is our teacher. Two more young Flyers are with me. What I learned there saved me last night. Otherwise, the War Flyers would have killed me for sure." She looked at Timo for a few moments. She saw some resentment and concern in his eyes. He played nervously with his hands and tried to avoid eye contact. "Are you going to help me?" Val asked carefully.

"Help you with what?" Timo asked in return. Her question had interrupted his thoughts.

"Rescuing my baby brother."

"You don't even know if he is in danger."

"Haven't you been listening to me?" Val responded angrily. "First they say he is dead, then they bring him to the Mountain of Glory, very much alive, where six Elders examine him while War Flyers in full armor are flying all around!" She jumped from Timo's bed and started to pace angrily up and down.

"Are you sure it was your brother you heard?" asked Timo.

Val stopped pacing as if hit by lightning. She turned around and looked at Timo with angry eyes, then said slowly, choosing each word carefully, "I heard him cry and recognized him. I felt him there! I felt my brother."

Timo swallowed then said quickly, "I would like to help you, but tomorrow evening I have to be at the Mountain of Clouds."

"At the Mountain of Clouds? You? Why?"

"I was summoned to appear in front of the Council."

"What have you done? Are you in trouble?"

"Yes, I think so. I jumped off the Cliff," Timo said, his head lowered.

"You did what?" Val said in disbelief. "You jumped off the Cliff and survived it? No one as young as you has ever done that. Not even Aldor, and I've heard that he was quite wild during his teen years."

"Maybe. They might forbid me to fly for a year, maybe even two years."

"Forbid you to fly! No!" Val yelled. "I need you. You are my only hope."

"I'm sorry," Timo said quietly. He got up from his bed slowly and walked towards Val who stood in disbelief beside the window. He took her hand. "We will find a way, but why not let Aldor know?" Timo asked.

"I don't know where he is, and he is an adult and a member of the Council. He might not believe me."

"I will see him tomorrow evening. I can talk to him then. Can you find out more about the Mountain of Glory and what is happening inside the library, more about your baby brother and what they want to do with him?" Timo asked.

"I could go back there tonight," Val said eagerly, hope shining in her eyes. "After last night's encounter, there might be more War Flyers there, but I will try it." Her mood was positive again; she was relieved she had found someone she could trust and who would help her.

"Do you think Aldor will listen to you?"

"I don't know. He will be busy defending me, I think. I will try."

"Thank you, Timo," Val said.

"You honor me with your trust," Timo responded, smiling at Val. "I thank you for that." Val smiled back at him. "Be careful tonight. From what you have told me, it seems that in order to keep their secret the War Flyers are willing to kill other Flyers."

Val stepped closer to him and gave him a gentle hug and a quick, shy kiss on his cheek, then she turned around and left silently and quickly. She didn't see Timo blush.

CHAPTER FOUR

Val's Brother

Val returned to her Mother's room in the northern wing of the Halls of Healing.

"You are back," her mother greeted her. "The Healing Flyer was just here. She said I can go home tomorrow."

"Are you sure? Isn't it a bit too soon?" Val asked, concerned. She sat on the edge of her mother's bed.

"It will be good for me," Val's mother said, trying to reassure Val. "If I stay here, I will just think and brood about what might have been." Her mother's eyes were filled with tears. "Your father was here earlier and I told him to pick me up tomorrow. He is very worried. He will be back later. Will you stay with me tonight?"

"Yes, I will, but don't wait for me. I have to do something. I will be by your side later."

"What will you be doing?"

"I met a boy from my school here. He has injured himself. I will try to help him."

"Using your healing talent? As you have done so many times with injured animals?" A small smile crossed her mother's face. "Who is he?"

"His name is Timo."

"The son of the murdered Rescue Flyer? He is a kind boy."

"Yes. He is already in pain, so what we're going to do will not hurt him much more. Rest now. I will see you later." Looking at her mother Val wondered, *What is going through your mind, Mother?* Wishing she could tell her mother her son was alive, Val kissed her softly on the forehead before leaving her room. She walked out of the building, drawn towards the

41

waterfall she had seen from Timo's room. She crossed a grassy field covered with blue and yellow flowers and sat down beside a small pool of mountain water, which collected here before flowing along the cliff and down to the next plateau. The meeting with Timo had cheered her up tremendously and had given her new hope. Deep inside she knew the two of them would rescue her brother. Listening to the songs of the mountain birds, Val felt at peace for the time being. She watched the mist that surrounded the waterfall and noticed how the wind pushed it up and down, sideways and in circles. She stored this observation in her mind together with the sound the wind was making while it played with the mist. One day she might use that knowledge while flying on a rainy day.

The previous night had been more dangerous than she had anticipated. The War Flyers' arrows had come very close, too close for her comfort. She had thought she'd scanned the area carefully. *What could I have done better?* Val wondered. The Rescue Flyers always debriefed after a mission or a close encounter so they could learn from any mistakes they might have made, but Val couldn't think of anything she had done wrong. She remembered, however, that on her way through the Halls of Healing she had seen two Flyers all bandaged up in one of the rooms close to where Timo was resting. War Flyer uniforms had hung over two chairs. *The two War Flyers. They are still alive,* she thought. *At least I don't have to worry I caused their deaths.*

The thought about death brought her mind back to her mother and brother. A sudden urge made her turn around and walk back to the Halls of Healing. Clouds began to drift in from the East and the sky became dark. Val returned to her mother's room to find her up and walking around. Val's mother smiled and gave her daughter a warm hug.

"I have good news," she said, tears of happiness in her eyes.

"What is it, Mother?" Val asked softly.

"Your brother. He is alive. Two Healing Flyers took him to the Mountain of Glory where the Elders examined him. He wasn't dead. He was in a deep sleep with his heart beating very slowly. The Elders were able to revive him." She started to laugh, filled with joy. She hugged Val again then danced enthusiastically around the room. Val was so happy to see her mother's joy, but confused about what she was hearing and intrigued to find out what was really happening. "He will come back to us within the month. He will stay with the Elders until he has fully recovered and is strong enough to return. Isn't that wonderful?"

"Yes, . . . yes, that is wonderful," Val replied absentmindedly, "but what are you doing?"

"Packing. I am going home today. The Mountain of Wind is waiting for me and your father is expecting us back. I am so happy."

"Will everything be fine with my brother, then?" Val asked carefully.

"Yes, that is what they said."

"Will he be able to fly?"

"Of course. Why do you ask?" Her mother looked at her daughter, concerned by her question.

"Oh nothing, just something I learned at school. Sometimes when babies have problems after birth their wings might not grow fully," she lied. "At least that is what they told us at school."

"He is perfectly fine. Two legs, two arms and two beautiful wings, that is what the Healing Flyer told me."

Val didn't want to ask any more questions, concerned she might give herself away. She helped her mother pack and prepare to fly back home. Just as they were finishing, a Healing Flyer came by to advise them it would be too dangerous to fly that night. The clouds had moved into the mountains, and the winds were strong. A storm was coming with thunder and lightning.

Excellent, Val thought. *No one will dare to be outside tonight. I will fly to the Mountain of Glory under the cover of the storm.*

Val's mother was so happy she didn't think twice when Val excused herself for a little while. Her mother simply smiled.

By the time Val had changed into her black outfit, the night had come and the wind was howling around the Halls of Healing. She quickly and silently passed by Timo's room where he was already asleep, exhausted from his exercises.

"See you later, my friend," she whispered.

Outside the air was cold and moist, and the wind hugged her tightly like a long lost friend. No matter how strong or soft, how tender or rough, how warm or cold, Val loved the wind. She opened her wings and was swooped away, quickly disappearing, unnoticed, into the night.

Her black cloak protected her from the cold and wet. She rushed towards the Mountain of Glory.

Tonight, no one will detect or follow me, Val thought.

She landed softly on the plateau and was inside the library quickly, her soft, leather shoes not making a sound. She sneaked along the wall toward the heavy wooden door. Nothing moved inside, everything was quiet and calm. The few burning candles gave Val enough light to find her way. Her heart was pounding with excitement. She felt exhilarated.

She opened the wooden door, whisked inside and crossed the polished floor. Something was pulling her forwards; an invisible force was guiding her. Val stopped for a while and listened. Nothing but the wind's song was audible. She moved beyond the next door and stood in another hallway with three doors at the end.

This is not a library, she thought, *this is a labyrinth.*

Slowly, but impatiently, she hunched forward, stopped, listened again. She looked at the three doors, crouched down and waited. There it was again, the invisible force pulling on her. She was ready to move through the left door when she heard voices, muffled, angry voices from behind the right door. She leaned carefully forward and pressed her ear against its cold surface.

"How dare you accuse me, Wardor."

"Two of my War Flyers were killed," Wardor lied, "by the spy who came out of your house last night. You owe me an explanation."

That is a lie, Val thought. *Those War Flyers are alive in the Halls of Healing. I didn't kill anyone. What is Wardor up to?*

"I don't owe you anything. You might be Lord of the War Flyers, but that doesn't give you any right or power to question the action of the Elders. Now leave!"

"I speak for all the Flyers when I question you. You are collaborating with our enemies, the Wanderers. I have watched for many years now and you cannot hide any longer. You and those useless Rescue Flyers. The spy must be one of them. The way he flew . . . only one who has the gift can escape the claws of the cold downdraft. I know what you are up to and I will expose your betrayal. You will be judged and thrown down the Cliff with your wings bound. Where is the baby?"

"You are as foolish as your father was, and if you don't leave immediately I will tell you more about your warmongering ancestors. Don't tempt me or I will expose you for what you really are."

"You will pay for your insults, old Flyer," Wardor yelled, then stormed across the room and kicked the door open so hard it crashed against the wall. He rushed out into the hallway, his black cloak waving furiously behind him.

In the meantime, Val had rushed through one of the other doors and was hiding behind it. She held her breath and didn't move an inch until the halls became quiet again. The more she heard and learned, the more confused she became. *What is the lord of the War Flyers talking about? The Wanderers are our sworn enemies. And why is he asking about my brother? Why is the Elder not telling him the truth about the baby? What is going on?*

When it seemed safe enough, Val got up and moved down the stairs in front of her. At the bottom she turned right into another room. In the center stood two small beds, and in one corner a chair on which a Healing Flyer was sleeping peacefully. A table stood between the beds. On it were two baby bottles filled with liquid. No other furniture decorated the room. The walls were painted white and the floor was made of black tile. Silently Val moved closer to the small beds. She looked into each one of them and thought, *Two babies. How is this possible?*

She knew instinctively which baby was her brother. When she looked into his bed, two bright, friendly blue eyes smiled at her. The force that had pulled her here was especially strong in his presence.

"Brother," she whispered, and the baby smiled. *The power of blood. That is what pulled me toward you.* She carefully lifted him out of bed and held him in her arms. Fearfully, she moved her hand across his small back. *No wings. The old law! I had almost forgotten about it. What shall I do? They will kill him.*

She held him out in front of her and gave him a big smile. "No wings," she whispered. "My brother, you are a Wanderer. For that I love you even more." Her heart filled with joy and pride when she looked at him, and a strange feeling rushed through her body, a feeling she had had before when she was very, very young, a feeling of being one with the Wanderers. Tears ran down her cheeks and the baby's little hands moved forward to touch them. Val smiled, gently kissed her baby brother on his forehead then put him back in his bed.

She leaned over the next small bed and lifted the other baby into her arms. She stroked the baby's back carefully. *No wings either. Two Wanderers have been born in the Mountains.* She carefully placed the baby back into bed and turned her attention to her brother again.

"I can't take you with me tonight, the wind is too strong, but I will return for you and get you back home where you belong, with us, our family. I will find you again, now that I know. I promise. I will not leave you in the hands of those who believe in that old, brutal, ridiculous law."

She left the room and ran back up the stairs. As she was closing the door behind her, she heard one of the babies begin to cry. It was her brother calling for her, begging her not to leave him behind. The crying pierced her heart and she wanted to go back. She was about to turn around when she heard the Healing Flyer get up and walk toward the baby's bed. "Don't cry, my little baby," a friendly voice cooed. "Come, let me cradle you. You must be hungry."

Val waited until she heard her baby brother settle down, then ran towards the big, wooden doors.

The full force of the storm howling around the plateau greeted Val outside. She ran to the mountain edge, opened her wings and was picked up vigorously by the hands of the howling wind. She momentarily lost control, freefalling down the mountain, but recovered quickly. "I couldn't have taken you with me," she whispered. "We wouldn't have survived this."

A shadow moved behind one of the building's windows. An Elder had watched the spy fly away. He turned around slowly and sat back down in his chair. Gazing into the huge fireplace he watched as the last flames slowly died away.

"I think we have reached a point in time when our secret is no longer safe," said Air. He breathed in heavily and looked at the two other Elders, Wind and Earth. They, too, were watching the small fire.

"What we have feared for the longest time is here now, staring us in the face," Wind said. "We've been lucky to be able to fool Wardor's spies for the last six years. Unfortunately, we have not been so lucky this time."

"This was not one of Wardor's spies," Air corrected him. "This spy has blonde hair and has the gift. Tomorrow evening the Council will meet to decide what to do with that impatient Flyer named Timo. He is the one we have been waiting for. He has the strength of his father, and the gift is glowing bright and strong inside of him. After meeting with the Council we must sit down with those we trust and who have served us without doubting our decisions," Air said.

"They deserve to be informed and to be asked for their advice," Earth added. "They are the alliance and they understand."

"So it is said, so it is done," Air concluded.

When the last flame had gone out, the three Elders got up and walked heavy heartedly to their rooms.

CHAPTER FIVE

The Mountain of Clouds

Timo continued his exercises. He did push-ups, sit-ups, and deep breathing. He especially stretched his wings and muscles. The exercises were less painful the more he did them, but they still brought tears to his eyes. He continued until his body was covered with sweat. He worked out for two more hours, until the sun shone brightly through his window. A desire to go outside and feel the wind again suddenly overcame him.

Walking along the white, long corridors, he passed by a room in which he saw two torn and dirty, black uniforms lying across two chairs. He backed up to have a closer look. *War Flyer uniforms*, he thought. *These must be the two War Flyers Val was talking about. So they are alive. Good. I have to tell Val. She will be happy to find out that they have survived their crash.*

In the next room he saw Rare talking to a Flyer with his right leg in a cast; Timo wondered what might have happened to that poor fellow.

Finally he reached the wooden door, slipped out of the Halls of Healing and stepped out into the sun. A warm breeze touched him and he closed his eyes to focus on the feeling it gave him. The wind, his friend, greeted him with a happy song.

"Open your wings and let me lift you, or are you too frightened to go on a ride?" the wind teased. "The air is fresh and I will hold you." Timo opened his eyes and smiled. "Come on, my friend. I will be your guide," the wind continued to sing.

"Where were you when I jumped off the Cliff?" Timo protested.

"Would you have listened?" the wind replied. "One can't stop a foolish person who has made up his silly mind."

Timo wanted to defend himself, but he knew the wind was right. He hadn't listened to his best friend, he hadn't listened to his instinct about the cold downdraft, and he wouldn't have listened to the wind either. He had been driven by his desire to prove himself worthy. Somehow he had to overcome his insecurity, but he didn't know how.

"You are right, my friend, like always," Timo blew into the air.

"Let me carry you, then," answered the wind.

Timo opened his wings ever so slowly while the wind carefully caressed them just enough to help Timo feel them open a little at a time until they were fully stretched. Timo could feel his feet leaving the ground. He hovered a few inches above the ground for a full minute before he folded his wings again and drifted back down, exhausted.

"Thank you, Wind, my friend," he whispered, "but I have to gain more strength before I can ride with you."

"You know where you can find me," the wind answered.

While Timo walked towards the waterfall he noticed dark clouds approaching the mountain from the east and felt a thunderstorm coming his way. *Val wanted to fly to the Mountain of Glory tonight,* he thought. *I hope she will be all right.* He sensed her presence as though she were standing beside him. He did not know she had stood right there just an hour before.

The cold mist of the waterfall surrounded him and he stepped forward into the falling water. The freezing water splashed across his body and ran down his head. He breathed in its freshness and enjoyed its chill on his skin. He thought of Val and worried about the adventure that lay ahead of her. He liked Val and missed her. He hoped he would see her again soon.

The skin on Timo's toes and fingers was wrinkled and blue when he finally stepped out of the waterfall. The wind was howling and the dark clouds blocked the sun. He returned to the Halls of Healing. The place was now busy with Healing Flyers who complained about the trail of wet footsteps Timo was leaving behind on the floor. He apologized politely, quickened his steps and vanished into his room. The white linen seemed to welcome him as he crawled into his bed. It hugged him closely and he felt his cold, shivering body begin to warm up. The evening came quickly; a Healing Flyer served him a light meal of fruits, vegetables, and rye bread, just enough to quiet his rumbling stomach and strengthen his muscles.

Although he fell asleep right away, Timo stirred throughout the night with the feeling that someone was watching him. Too tired to open his eyes, he smelled a foul aroma he thought he knew but couldn't identify. The next moment it was gone.

The following morning began the same way as the day before and the day before that. Rare woke him with her happy voice, and he was glad to see her. The exercises went well; Rare was proud of Timo and the progress he was making.

"Tonight you will be able to fly to the Mountain of Clouds," she said.

"I hope I will be strong enough to fly the distance by myself," Timo replied sincerely. "I was told I have to go alone. I am concerned my penalty will be severe."

"You will be fine, Aldor is on your side," Rare reassured him.

"I know, but I have to fly. They can't take that away from me. It is like water for a fish, like air for the living, you know what I mean?"

"I have an idea, but I will never fly with your wings. You are strong, as strong as your father was. I helped him once, when he crashed."

"My father crashed?" Timo smiled. "I didn't know that."

"Yes, it was during the storm season. Your father ended up in a cold downdraft and had a close encounter with a tree. Luckily nothing was broken, but one of his wings was very badly bruised, almost like yours."

"Thank you for telling me," Timo said.

"Believe in yourself. You have the gift that only a special few have. Be strong and face the Council with pride, but be careful because one Flyer will watch you very closely."

"I think I know who you mean. Wardor?" Timo asked.

"Yes. He has no mercy and he doesn't like those who have the gift."

"Who are those two Flyers in the other room?" Timo asked, even though he already knew the answer.

"They are War Flyers who crashed. They were chasing a spy who was hanging around the Mountain of Glory," Rare answered.

"War Flyers and spies on the Mountain of Glory?"

"Yes, strange things have been happening lately," Rare replied, then left the room.

Timo sat on his bed and thought about his meeting with the Council. He was anxious and nervous and couldn't wait for the day to come to an end, but he hoped Val would come by to tell him what she had discovered on the Mountain of Glory. He stood up from his bed and paced nervously about his room. He had just begun his exercises again and was preparing mentally for the meeting when a friendly face looked around the corner.

"Val, come in," he said jubilantly, excited to see her again. "What happened?"

"It is terrible," Val replied, her head lowered as she entered. "I found my brother and held him. He is beautiful, wonderful, amazing. He is a Wanderer."

"What do you mean?" Timo asked, horrified. He hated Wanderers.

"He has no wings, but I can feel him as if we were one. His blood also flows in my veins, but I am not a Wanderer. Or am I?" Val looked at her hands absentmindedly. She turned them over and around as if looking for something.

"You are a Flyer. You have wings. You were born in the Mountains," Timo replied, walking closer to Val. "The Wanderers are savages, killers and the enemies of the Flyers. You have no connection with them."

"How would you know? My brother was born by a Flyer, but he is a Wanderer, and I feel him like I have never felt anybody else before. I am drawn to him." Val began to cry silently. "I have to rescue him!" She said suddenly, and stretched herself tall, almost as tall as Timo.

"You don't know if he is in any danger. Maybe they're just keeping him for observation."

"Have you forgotten about the old law? '**Those born without wings have to die!**' Remember? I have to rescue him or they will kill him."

"They wouldn't kill a baby!" Timo replied, enraged. "The Rescue Flyers wouldn't allow it."

"Wardor was on the Mountain of Glory in the old library," Val replied coldly. "He is the strongest supporter of the old laws. He would kill his own parents if they violated any of those stupid, old laws."

Timo was quiet. He knew about the reputation of the ruthless leader of the War Flyers and he knew Wardor would not hesitate when it came to maintaining the old laws. He would be capable of killing a baby.

"Will you help me?" Val pleaded.

Timo looked into her begging eyes; he felt helpless. What was he supposed to do? "I . . . I," he began and swallowed. He steadied himself and finally said, "I have to go and face the Council. If I don't go, they might clip my wings. I will help you, I want to help, but I have to do this first, do you understand?"

Val didn't. She felt as if a cold blade had penetrated her heart. She was alone. She shivered slightly and looked away from Timo's closely watching eyes.

"I understand," she whispered, then turned around and ran out of the room.

"Val!" Timo yelled. "Wait!" But Val was gone.

*** *** ***

When he saw the sun standing above the Mountain of Winds, Timo knew it was time for him to get ready. He was thinking about Val and was feeling really bad, but what could he do? If he lost the opportunity to fly he would be no good to anybody.

The Healing Flyers had repaired and cleaned his uniform, and it was hanging over the single chair that stood in the corner of his white room. He quickly put it on, walked through the hallways and out the front door onto the mountain plateau. Nobody saw him leave.

"Hello," the soft, warm wind greeted him. The storm from the previous night had passed and the evening was calm and pleasantly mild.

"Hello, my friend," Timo responded. The wind was playing softly with his long, brown curls. "Please help me soar up high to the Mountain of Clouds." He opened his wings and jumped into the air. The wind picked him up and supported him carefully. Timo moved his wings up and down and formed a V with his legs. He turned slowly until he faced the Mountain of Clouds. His muscles were listening to him, but only under protest and pain. Timo moved his wings faster and flew to his meeting.

With clenched teeth and sweat running down his back Timo landed in front of the house of the Council. He was surprised how easy it had been to find, despite the thick clouds. He walked toward the massive wooden door that would lead him inside the brick mansion. The leaded glass windows of the house were large and threatening. Gargoyles were mounted along the roof and above the entrance. A heavy iron bar shaped like a hammer hung in the center of the door. He lifted the hammer and knocked. The banging sound echoed throughout the house and a dark, frightening voice shouted, "Who is there?"

Timo stepped away from the door and replied loudly and defiantly, "My name is Timo. I am from the Mountain of Wind and I am here by request of the Council."

"Timo. Yes. The Council is waiting for you."

The door creaked opened and Timo walked inside. An elderly Flyer stood in front of Timo, looking at him with a friendly, almost fatherly smile. The Elder was slightly hunched over and had a grey beard outlining his wrinkled face. He offered his hand in greeting. Timo walked up to him, lowered his head, and took the hand as a sign of acceptance. Old, cold fingers curled around Timo's hand so Timo was surprised by the strong handshake that followed.

"Welcome, Timo of the Mountain of Wind, Cliff diver," the Elder said. "My name is Air. I am the oldest of the three Elders who guide the Council. Please follow me. Everyone is here and ready."

"Thank you, Air," Timo responded.

Air turned quickly and led the way through the old house. He wore a purple robe with a golden belt, and he was half a head taller than Timo, who followed him silently. They walked through a narrow corridor, turned left and stood in front of another door which was painted black and covered with burgundy colored tiles. Without hesitation, Air opened the door and walked into a barely lit room. The room had tall, vaulted ceilings; large tapestries covered the walls, and the floor was made of red hardwood. A large, round table with a hole in its center stood in the middle of the room. Ten chairs made of rosewood, their seats covered with dark blue velvet fabric, were placed equidistantly around the table. Each chair was engraved with the emblem of a different Flyer group. A chair covered with red velvet fabric stood in the center of the round table.

"Please move to the center of the table," Air directed Timo. When Timo looked confused, Air added, "Just fly there."

Timo clenched his teeth, moved his wings up and down then flew over the table. He was just about to sit down in the red chair when Air gave him an angry look.

"Don't sit," he said harshly. "Wait for the Council to arrive."

"I am sorry," Timo apologized fearfully. He stood on the platform beside the chair.

Air turned around and walked toward another door. He smiled to himself and thought, *I really like this boy. He is strong and determined, but still has respect for his elders.* Air knocked at the door with three long knocks followed by two short ones. He returned to the table and sat down on the chair that had a cloud engraving on its back. The door opened and seven Flyers, one wolf, and one eagle walked into the room. Air introduced them individually as they sat down in their chairs.

"To my right is Wind, the second Elder, also known as the Wise One." Timo saw a circle with a bar across it on the back of Wind's chair.

"To my left is Earth, the third Elder, also known as the Scientific One." A pyramid with an eye in it was Earth's emblem. With each introduction the platform on which Timo stood turned so that he faced the Elder being introduced. Timo looked into the eyes of each Elder and bowed respectfully.

"Beside Earth is Stodor, Lord of the Storm Flyers." Stodor wore a silver cloak, and Timo saw a zigzag arrow engraved in his chair. The platform shifted again.

"Beside him is Raidor, Lord of the Rain Flyers." A simple, five-pointed star was Raidor's emblem, and he wore a dark blue cloak.

"Followed by Aldor, Lord of the Rescue Flyers." Two wings were engraved in Aldor's chair, and he wore a dark yellow cloak. Timo looked at him and smiled, relieved. *One friendly face I know*, he thought, but Aldor gave him a stern, serious look, not showing any sign of knowing him. Timo bowed his head.

Next was a tall, skinny Flyer who looked at Timo with wise eyes. "Dodor," Air announced, "Lord of the Healing Flyers."

The platform moved again and Air continued, "Wardor, Lord of the War Flyers." Timo bowed then looked up into one cold, grey, emotionless eye. The other eye was covered with a black patch. A long sword was carved in Wardor's chair, and he wore a black cloak.

Next, Timo looked into the crystal blue eyes of a large, black timber wolf. He knew him from an encounter in the Wolf Forest. He had walked into the forest one day to see the young pups play. This wolf had stopped the others from killing him.

Air explained, "This is the lord of Wolf Forest, protector of the forests and mountains. He wants to be named Wolf, for what he is." Timo bowed respectfully. The platform moved again.

"Eagle, Lord of the Skies and protector of the Mountain of Clouds." A majestic, brown eagle stood in front of Timo, staring at him with calm yellow eyes.

The platform moved for the last time and Timo faced Air again. "My name is Air. I am the first Elder, Head of the Council, also known as the Seer. My symbol is the . . . ."

"Enough of these overused pleasantries," Wardor interrupted rudely. His voice was rough and sharp as a knife. Timo felt a cold chill run down his back as the platform moved him to face the lord of the War Flyers again.

"Sit," Wardor yelled at him. "You are here because of your stupid, irresponsible stunt that not only endangered you but others as well."

"No one else was in any danger," Aldor said calmly. "What he did was foolish, not stupid or irresponsible."

"No surprise that you protect this little misfit since he is your friend's son," Wardor said angrily.

"We all know you lack patience and compassion, Wardor, but I didn't know that you are ignorant too," Aldor responded, holding Wardor's enraged stare. "Nonetheless, that doesn't give you the right to be rude, or to unfairly accuse me. Timo's father was my friend, everyone knows that, but that doesn't influence my integrity, objectivity, or responsibility to this council. Never suggest the contrary," Aldor's voice boomed.

The two Flyers stared at each other coldly; their eyes were filled with hatred toward one other.

"In any case, he broke the rules by jumping off the Cliff without permission," Wardor stated emphatically. "The Cliff has a special meaning to all of us and you, Aldor, should know that best."

"I know, and you, especially you, don't have to remind me," Aldor responded.

Timo sensed the tension between the two Flyers. They definitely weren't friends. Eventually the other Flyers entered the conversation and added their thoughts to the discussion, except Air who was watching Timo intently. Timo seemed to be reacting to all the words, accusations, charges, and hatred he was confronted with. Air could sense anger, frustration and sadness coming from Timo.

The platform continued to rotate, so Timo was able to look into the eyes of each Flyer as he spoke. He felt sympathy and understanding coming from all except Wardor. Wardor's words were mean and degrading, malicious and unfair. Timo didn't fear him, though he should have since Wardor hated those who had the gift and had thought often about how to get rid of all the Rescue Flyers. Wardor had already killed one Flyer in cold blood, from behind, one of the finest and best. This was something no one else knew.

Finally, Air stood up and said, "Enough." Timo stood up as well, remembering Air's earlier instruction. "Please, Timo, sit," Air said with an appreciative smile. "Enough said. The night has taken over the day and the stars are shining brightly. What do you say, Wardor?"

"Two years without flying and two additional years in the service of the Council. What he did was outrageous and undisciplined. He needs to be punished, and punished he will be!" Wardor's grey eye glittered with anger and hatred.

Timo's eyes filled with tears. "Four years without flying? That's not possible. I couldn't," he said.

"Silence," Air said angrily and gave Timo a stern look. "You were not addressed and so should not speak."

Timo lowered his head in shame, but his anger and frustration grew stronger.

"Aldor, what do you say?" Air asked. He had heard the panic and pain in Timo's voice but he had to be tough, even though Timo had regretted his outburst right away.

"What Timo did shows what he is capable of doing. We can't punish him because he has the gift and is impatient. We can't take away what will be of great value to all of us one day. Timo has to fly. But he has to learn to be patient. I suggest Timo stay with me. I am willing to take full responsibility for him and his actions. He will come with me to the Mountain of Sun and train with the other selected Flyers."

"No way," Wardor bellowed. "That is no punishment, it is a reward. This is outrageous!"

"Quiet, Wardor," Air said angrily. "You had your turn to talk, now is your time to listen. Your behavior is not becoming of a lord. Aldor, please continue."

"Thank you, Air. As a penalty I suggest that Timo join the Maintenance Flyers and clean the school during the summer break. He will clean walls, scrub floors, wash windows and all the blackboards, and mop the bathrooms."

Hearing this Timo's mood improved and his hope increased.

"Stodor, what do you say?"

"I agree with Aldor. Timo survived a foolish act, which promises him a bright future if he is guided well. No untrained Flyer has ever survived the Cliff."

"Raidor?"

"I agree with Wardor. We can't tolerate such arrogant, self-serving behavior. Timo must be punished severely, otherwise others will see his act as admirable and will wish to imitate him."

"Yes," Wardor yelled, smashing his fist on the table. "I am not the only one who believes in our rules."

"Restrain yourself, Wardor," Air shouted, angrier than before. "This is a Council meeting and not one of your war camps."

"Dodor, what do you say?"

"Aldor is right, but I would like to suggest that Timo also help out in the Halls of Healing so he can learn about the pain of others, not physical pain, but pain of the heart and of the mind. Learning compassion and understanding for the lives and feelings of his fellow Flyers is important."

"Wolf, what do you say?"

"Our young ones learn by watching and trying. If they don't take chances they will not learn. We should be proud of Timo for what he has risked. It shows bravery, determination, and strength. In my opinion, he shouldn't be punished at all."

"Eagle, what do you say?"

"Timo overstepped his boundaries. Those who live in the Mountains have to follow the established rules, otherwise our community will end in chaos. If Aldor can teach him that, then I support Aldor's suggestion."

Air looked at both of the other Elders and they nodded in agreement.

"So be it," he said. "Timo will live with Aldor under his guidance and rules. Aldor will be responsible for all of Timo's future actions. Timo will help the Maintenance Flyers as often as possible, and he will meet with Dodor once a week to help out in the Halls of Healing. As an additional request, I would like to see Timo every two weeks to evaluate his progress. This is what I say. This is what is decided. Let this be written down in the Book of Statements."

Timo stood up and the platform slowly rotated. He bowed in front of each Council member as each rose and said, "So it is said, so it is done." All spoke, except one.

"You may go now, Timo," Air said.

"Thank you," Timo said, smiling with relief. He opened his wings and flew across the table toward Aldor who was already standing by the door.

"Fly home, Timo," Aldor said. "Your mother is waiting for you."

"Thank you, Aldor. Thank you for everything."

"I will see you tomorrow afternoon on the Mountain of Sun. Find Val, she knows the way, and also get your friend Dino. I have to talk with him. Tell him to bring the four books, he will know which ones." He put his hand on Timo's shoulder and smiled.

Timo looked at Aldor and blushed. He was overcome with a sense of guilt and panic. *Val,* he thought. *Where is Val?*

CHAPTER SIX

Home

The night had arrived before Timo had found his way home. His only guide had been the flames of a fire that glowed in the open pit in the backyard of his home. His mother had lit the signal fire many times before when he had been late coming home. She was waiting beside it when Timo finally arrived. He walked up to her and she pulled him close, embracing him. She cried quietly on his shoulder.

"I'm sorry, Mother," Timo whispered.

"I love you so much," she replied. She was furious and angry, but also happy and relieved she was holding her son in her arms again. "I don't know what I would do if I lost you, too. Don't you ever do this to me again," she said quietly, trying to keep her voice from trembling.

"You won't lose me. I love you."

"Come inside. You must be hungry. The food at the Halls of Healing isn't enough for a growing flyer." Her anger was gone, but her worries still lingered.

They walked arm in arm into the small house. Timo sat down at the table that was set with fresh bread, grapes, sausages, cheese, scrambled eggs, and his favorite, warm broccoli. He ate hastily and with appetite while telling his mother what had happened. He told her about Rare, the Healing Flyer who had tortured him with kindness. He also told her about Aldor, the meeting with the Elders, and the hatred he felt coming from Wardor. He didn't tell her about Val's baby brother. He trusted his mother, but he thought his own story was enough to take in for one night. After meeting with the Council, Timo had returned to the Halls of Healing to look for Val, but he had been told that she and her mother had left for home that evening. He had felt somewhat relieved, but an uneasy feeling had accompanied him on his flight home.

"I will be guided by Aldor," he continued, feeling his mother's stare.

"I know," his mother said calmly. "He came by yesterday and asked me for my permission, which I gladly gave him. You need the guidance of an experienced Flyer who understands your gift and who can deal with it."

"Thank you, Mother."

Before he went to bed, Timo's mother said, "Val was here a couple of times, asking for you. She seemed nervous and excited. Did you know she had a baby brother who will be coming home in a few weeks?"

"Yes, I met her on the Mountain of Life. That is wonderful news. Good night, Mother."

"Good night, Timo," she said and kissed him on his cheek. "Don't scare me like that again."

"I will try my best, but you know me Mother."

"Yes, I do. That is why I am so concerned. You better listen to Aldor. If I hear anything, just the tiniest remark that you might have done something dangerous, I will ground you for two months. Now, sleep well." She took him in her arms again and gave him a loving kiss on his cheek.

Timo walked upstairs thinking about Val. *I wonder what happened. Maybe Val was wrong and the Elders healed her baby brother? I can't wait until I see her tomorrow. We will fly to the Mountain of Sun, together.* Smiling, he fell fast asleep, despite the pain in his wings.

*** *** ***

The three Elders walked toward the upper level of the meeting hall. They had asked Aldor, Dodor, Wolf, and Eagle to join them after the Council meeting. It was time to discuss the future with their allies.

"Thank you for coming," Air greeted them after sitting down in the small living room.

"What a meeting and what a courageous, brave young Flyer that Timo is. Impatient, but the gift is strong in him. Stronger than it is in you, Aldor, or than it was in his father."

"Yes, Air," Aldor said. "I have great hope for him. He is our future."

"Now let's talk about the reason we've asked you to meet with us so late. Wardor is getting more suspicious, and we think he knows what is going on. However, he has no proof. When Timo's father was killed, Wardor nearly discovered the truth. In addition to this, a spy has entered these halls and has seen the babies without wings."

"A Rescue Flyer," Wind added, "a blonde haired Rescue Flyer." He looked at Aldor, concerned.

"I think I know who it is," Aldor responded. "What do you suggest we do?"

"Who is the spy?" Air asked.

"Her name is Val, an excellent Flyer. She was selected earlier this year to train on the Mountain of Sun. Her brother is in the halls of the library at the Mountain of Glory."

"Her brother?" Air continued.

"Yes. The baby brought here two days ago. The Wanderer is Val's brother. Val is a determined girl. Once she sets out to learning something she will not stop until she has satisfied her curiosity. She must have sensed her brother is still alive."

"I think she knows what her brother is," Air stated, concerned.

"I will have to talk to her, and to Timo, and invite them to join us. We have to tell them what is happening," Aldor said.

"Aren't they too young?" asked Dodor, Lord of the Healing Flyers. "Why would we tell them?"

"They already suspect something, and suspicion can lead to mistrust. We should be the ones who tell them," Aldor explained.

"I have watched Timo since he entered our forest," Wolf said. "He is a mature, young Flyer. The death of his father four years ago forced him to grow up quickly. He is ready for and will understand the truth."

"And Val?" asked Earth.

"She is more mature than many of the grade ten students. That is why she was chosen to join the selected ones," the Golden Eagle said. "I have been soaring with her many times. I caught her above the Mountain of Clouds when she was ten years old. When she saw me she tried to hide behind a tower cloud. When I asked her what she was doing and explained it was forbidden to fly there, she simply said she wanted to see the Hall of the Council. I asked her why she would risk her life just to see it and she replied, 'I wanted to see where the future is made and where justice is done.'"

The Golden Eagle looked at Aldor and said, "You will have your hands full with Val and Timo, but they are mature and I trust them. They are ready to learn what we have tried to hide for so long. I hope they are willing to join us."

"So be it. Aldor, it seems you will be carrying a heavy burden. We all rely on you," Air said. "Tell them the truth and invite them to join us. So it is said, so it is done.

"Now, what about Wardor? He has threatened the Elders," Aldor cautioned.

"He knows that Wanderers are being born to Flyers. He will not stop until he is in control of all the mountains. He will try to convince the rest of the Flyers that we are traitors trying to interfere with the way of life of the Flyers," explained Earth. "He will try to charge us with treason."

"He will not get away with it. What we are doing is just and morally correct," Dodor said. "We began this mission together when we realized what was happening six years ago. This development and change is good. It might unite all our people again, as we were before the Great War. Remember the words in the ancient statements?

And all the plains are filled with happiness and the mountains sing with joy; all people breathe the same air and share their food. We come together to celebrate the sun and the rain, embracing one another as brothers and sisters. The houses in the Mountains and the houses in the Flatlands are open to all visitors; trust is the basis of understanding and love. We, Wanderers and Flyers, are one people.

All who were present listened closely to Dodor's words. His dark voice sang the wisdom of the past, the wisdom of those who had written it down for others to remember.

"One day we will be one people again, Wanderers and Flyers living together in peace," Wind said. "The change that is happening is a sign. It cannot be reversed. We must continue with what we are doing until all are ready to understand. We cannot allow innocent babies, Wanderers or Flyers, to be killed."

"We have to tell the truth to all Flyers," Dodor said. "If they all know, then Wardor will have no influence over the Flyers."

"You are right," Air said, "but are the Flyers ready to learn the truth? Or will they panic?"

"We must begin with Val and Timo, and we must look after the babies. The ones in the Flatlands, the Wanderers we have contacted, are ready. Our allies there must become involved as well. The hatred among all our people is rooted very deep and it is kept alive by the likes of Wardor and the older Flyers. They cannot forgive. Being willing to sacrifice their own babies because of an outdated, ridiculous law shows what they are capable of," Aldor said.

"Dodor, you and two Healing Flyers will look after the two babies who are here. You have to bring them to our allies in the Flatlands. Explain the situation to them and wait for their response," Air summarized. "Wolf, you must send your spies to follow Wardor and find out what he is up to. We have reached a critical point in our mission. The next few weeks will be crucial to our future as a humane, civil people. Now go your ways. So it is said, so it is done."

All were standing when Aldor said, "Honor and loyalty. What we do is not for us, but for the future of all people."

CHAPTER SEVEN

The Mountain of Sun

"Timo," a young voice yelled. "Timo!"

Clong. A stone hit Timo's bedroom window.

"Timo."

Timo opened the shutters and looked down into the garden. "Yes. What?" he called. Val stood among his mother's flowerbeds, which shimmered in red, blue, and yellow. The flower petals were covered with a fine mist and water droplets sparkled in the early rays of the sun. "Come down. We have to talk," she said.

"The sun is barely up. What do you want to do?"

"Talk! Don't you listen?"

"Okay, give me a minute." Timo closed his window, dressed, stretched his stiff and aching wings and muscles, and walked downstairs. He grabbed a slice of bread, some cheese and salami, and went outside into the garden.

Val was standing below the old willow tree playing with her long, blonde hair. When she saw Timo she ran toward him, grabbed his hand and pulled him away from the house. She ran for a moment, dragging Timo behind her, then stopped abruptly when they'd reached the clearing from which they could see the Mountain of Glory. "Isn't that a great view, Timo! I love to look down into the Flatlands. The lake in the distance is so blue." Val continued talking excitedly. "I am glad to see you, finally. I was by your house several times last evening. What took you so long to get home? I was worried they'd thrown you into the dungeon. Are you all right?" she asked.

"I am fine," Timo replied, somewhat coldly. "But are you all right? The last time I saw you in the Halls of Healing you'd just left my room very upset with me. I remember your disappointment when I had to fly to the Council meeting instead of helping you."

"That was yesterday," she said with a smile. "Today is a new day." She was filled with excitement and life.

Timo was irritated and sensed something was wrong. He thought for a moment, then asked, "When is your brother coming home?"

"Soon," Val lied. She was still disappointed with Timo, but after what she had done the previous night, she was so proud of herself she couldn't hold her grudge against him.

I did it, she thought. *Alone. I didn't need anybody's help.*

"How can that be? Didn't you say he has no wings and you feared for his life?"

"I was mistaken," she lied again. One lie usually leads to another lie and Val's story was no exception. "I was at the mountain again," she continued, pointing at the Mountain of Glory. "I held my brother, and he is fine. Like I said, I was mistaken."

"Didn't you hear them say 'No wings'?" Timo asked.

"There were so many voices, I must have misunderstood."

They sat down in the grass and Timo argued, "What you've told me doesn't make any sense. Why don't they return your brother if he is fine?"

Val picked up a small branch and played with it, moving it between her fingers. "I don't know, but everything will be fine." She looked at Timo and smiled. "So what happened to you, Timo?"

Timo was surprised by the sudden question and couldn't respond right away. His thoughts were still with Val's baby brother. He refocused his thoughts and answered

70

enthusiastically, "I think I was lucky. Aldor defended me vehemently. The Council made the decision that Aldor will be my guardian and watch over me. I will join him on the Mountain of Sun to train with the selected ones, including you."

"I knew you would be fine," Val replied.

"How did you know?"

"I saw you in my mind standing among Elders and Lords in the center of a round table. I felt your relief when you heard Air's words," Val explained.

"How do you know about the round table?"

"I saw you, in my mind."

"How is that possible?"

"I don't know, but sometimes I have visions. Like when I saw my brother in the basement of the library before I flew to the Mountain of Glory, and when I saw you in the forest of the wolves before you'd even left to see the wolf puppies."

"Can you see the future?" Timo asked, his eyes wide with surprise.

"I don't know what it is, but it could be. Time will tell," she replied, then suddenly she had a vision of her brother dangling above the deadly abyss of the Cliff with a voice shouting, "The old laws will prevail!" A shiver ran down her back and she closed her eyes. She moved her trembling hands over her face to hide from Timo.

"Val?" Timo asked carefully. "Val, are you okay?"

"Yes," Val replied through a thick fog. She had to work hard to refocus her attention. Finally, in a stable voice she said, "Yes, I am fine." She lowered her hands and looked into Timo's worried eyes.

Suddenly Timo remembered what Aldor had said. "What time is it?" he asked.

"About ten," Val replied, still upset by her vision.

"That late? I have to be on the Mountain of Sun by noon. Aldor said to bring you since you know the way. It is too late to get Dino. Let's go."

Val let go of her dark thoughts and said a little too exuberantly, "Perfect. So we will be together. I am so happy. Come, let's go." She worked hard to push away the images that lingered in her mind. It was easier to do this when she told herself her brother was safe. *I made sure of that,* she thought.

Val jumped up, opened her wings, and was in the air before Timo could stand.

"Wait," Timo yelled. "There is more."

"Tell me on the way to the mountain."

Timo opened his wings and moved them slowly up and down before leaping into the air and being carried away by his friend the wind.

"So, what else?" Val asked when Timo had caught up with her.

The wind played with her long hair and she wore a beautiful smile. Timo felt comfortable around her.

"I have to work with the Maintenance Flyers and clean up the school during the summer break, plus I have to help out in the Halls of Healing. I also have to meet with Dodor once a week and with Air every two weeks."

"You were really lucky. That is hardly any punishment considering what you did."

"You sound like Wardor. If it had been up to him, I would never fly again." Timo protested.

"Wardor is dangerous. Aldor said so," Val replied seriously.

"What do you know about Wardor? He was furious, angry, and more than upset. I think he hates me." Val could hear the fear in Timo's voice.

Looked

"Don't worry. Wardor hates everyone. He would hate himself if he weren't so much in love with his reflection in the mirror," Val replied coldly.

Both laughed. Timo felt a warm glow whenever he heard Val's laughter. He had never felt like this with anyone else. He enjoyed her company and he enjoyed talking to her. At the same time, he could sense there was something she hadn't told him, something she was holding back, something that spoiled their innocent friendship. "What aren't you telling me?" he asked bluntly, without considering the consequences of his question.

Val looked at him for a while then asked, "How do you know?"

"I think there is something going on that you're not telling me."

They soared high above the Mountain of Wind. A warm updraft pushed them higher into the sky.

Val wasn't sure if Timo knew what she had really done the previous night or if it was something else. *I can't tell him*, she thought. "You are right," she said.

"Please tell me," Timo said softly.

"You saw Wardor's eye patch?"

"Yes."

"He lost his eye in a fight with your father. They were both seventeen years old when your father tried to stop Wardor from beating up a twelve-year-old boy. Wardor is basically a coward, so he is never alone. Two of his bully friends came from behind a tree and overwhelmed your father. They held him down while Wardor hit him in the face. Your father somehow freed himself and picked up a fallen branch to defend himself against the three cowards. When he managed to hit Wardor in the face the three of them ran away. They accused your father of ambushing Wardor and poking his eye out.

Luckily the twelve-year-old boy was brave enough to tell the Council what had really happened. That is why Wardor hates you so much."

"I see," said Timo. His heart smiled with pride. "Three against one. My father was brave and just."

Dear wind, I miss him so much, he thought. A cold breeze came down from the clouds and touched his face briefly as if responding to his very thought. Timo heard the wind say, "I miss him, too. He was the best Flyer and I loved lifting him."

"Who was the twelve-year-old boy?" Timo asked.

"It was Aldor. He told us the story. Wardor hates him, too."

"I thought so," Timo said.

"Come. Down there is the Mountain of Sun." Val took Timo's hand and they quickly flew down to the mountain.

*** *** ***

"Welcome," Aldor greeted them with a happy smile. "You are just in time. Before we start showing you around and begin your training, Timo, I have to talk to you two. Serious issues have arisen and I have to tell you what is going on. I know you must have many questions, especially the spy among you." He gave Val a serious look. "What I have to tell you may answer some of your questions. I trust you both. Please follow me, we have to go to a place where no one can hear us. What happened last night might have serious consequences." Aldor looked again at Val and she knew that she was in trouble.

CHAPTER EIGHT

Wardor

As soon as Wardor returned to his stronghold in the high mountains, west of the Five Mountains, he called for a meeting with his war council.

"They have fooled us long enough," he addressed his lieutenants angrily. "The Elders are weak and misguided and, worst of all, they listen to the Rescue Flyers, to that Aldor. What they are doing is treason, I know it, but cannot prove it yet. Four years ago we were so close, but we failed. We were hard on the trail of two Rescue Flyers, Aldor and Gildor. They were delivering something to the Wanderers, but they escaped thanks to their gift. We have to be ruthless to save our people. All Flyers depend on us."

"What happened at the Council meeting?" one of the lieutenants asked.

"The boy was not punished at all. That shows you what preferred treatment those with the gift get. Aldor will be his guardian and will look after him. It's a disgrace. Aldor knows the identity of the spy who nearly killed two of us, but he won't tell. He made a mockery of me and thus of all the War Flyers. If Gildor hadn't interfered years ago, I would have beaten that weakling Aldor to a pulp when he was young. I've had some revenge, though," Waldor added, laughing hysterically.

"So tell us about the boy. What is he like? Did he really jump from the Cliff and survive?" asked the first lieutenant with admiration and jealousy in his voice.

"Everyone knows he jumped and survived," Wardor replied angrily. "Timo is Gildor's gifted son, and Gildor is the one who used to be Lord of the Rescue Flyers, the one who took my eye, the one I killed because none of you were brave enough. The Elders say Timo is our future, those old fools. I am the future. The War Flyers are the future for these mountains, and we will rule," he yelled. His face was red with excitement. There were beads of sweat on his forehead. He was talking himself into a frenzy.

"All my ancestors fought the Wanderers, and my grandfather and father gave their lives to preserve our values. They fought so we could live prosperously. Now those Rescue Flyers and Elders want to throw it all away. No, I say. I will destroy those Flatlanders, together with those who stand in my way. They are traitors, no matter if they are Flyers. Our time has come. You, my friends and our people, are strong enough this time. No one will stop us."

He was breathing heavily. When he looked at his lieutenants he saw the gleam in their eyes; he reveled in their admiration.

"What are your orders, my Lord? We are ready to follow you," the first lieutenant said enthusiastically.

Wardor had surrounded himself with his closest confidants. All wore the traditional uniform of the War Flyers: a black cloak with a golden sword embroidered on the back.

"I know the Elders and their allies are in communication with the Wanderers. I don't know why, but I think it has something to do with the babies that have died in the past six years. All the spies I have sent have not been able to find out anything. I still don't know exactly what is going on. We have to do something drastic. We have to enter the old library on the Mountain of Glory. We have to enter the Halls of Healing on the Mountain of Life."

"But my Lord, isn't that forbidden? No one is allowed to enter without being invited by the elders, and no one is allowed in the Halls of Healing with weapons."

"The time has come. We have no choice. We must act. Send War Flyers to the library and to the Halls of Healing. I need spies on the Mountain of Sun to watch Aldor and Timo. Also, send War Flyers to the Mountain of Wind to watch over the other Flyers. This is it, the time is ours and I will no longer wait."

"It will be done as you say, my Lord."

"Kill those two failures who crashed to the ground," Wardor ordered. "We don't need them among us if they are not capable of killing a single Rescue Flyer." He rose from his chair and left the room, leaving his lieutenants behind to discuss the details of the operation. He knew he had convinced his Flyers. On the way to his room to rest, a voice in the dark stopped him.

"Well spoken." A shadow appeared from a dark corner.

"What are you doing here?" Wardor asked harshly. "What if someone sees you? You will turn me into a liar. Do you think we staged your state funeral so you can return whenever you want to? We need you dead so we can carry out our revenge and get the Flyers on our side."

"I had to come. I can no longer hide. My time is coming to an end soon. I can feel it. I found out something that will interest you very much."

"Follow me quickly, Grandpa," Wardor hushed. "Into my bedroom." Gustus slowly stepped out of the shadows and followed his grandson. He was hunched over and breathed heavily. "Sit down," Wardor said. "I told everyone you were killed by the Wanderers. You can't just appear."

"I had to. You have to destroy the Wanderers. You have to avenge your ancestors. You have to kill them, even those who are born among us."

"Born among us? What do you mean?"

"That is what the Elders have been doing, protecting the Wanderers who were born in the mountains. Those who were born by Flyers, born without wings." Gustus coughed violently.

"How is this possible?"

"I don't know." He coughed again and gasped for air. Blood trickled out of his mouth and down his chin. Wiping it away angrily with his cloak sleeve, he whispered, "Listen." Panic filled his broken voice, panic brought on by his vision of the approaching Death Flyer. "He is coming for me and I have to follow him! Before this happens I must tell you. It has happened seven times now that a Flyer has given birth to a Wanderer. Each time the Elders have made arrangements to bring them to the people of the Flatlands so the infants would not be killed. Everyone knows the law:

Those born without wings must prove they are worthy to live in the Mountains. Take them to the Cliff and offer them to the wind. If they are meant to fly, they will return.

My ancestors instituted that law and it is the legacy of our family. You must uphold the law. The Elders are weak and those Rescue Flyers are dangerous. Two Wanderers were born the other day, one in the Halls of Healing and one on the Mountain of Wind. They are now on the Mountain of Glory. Find them and you will have your proof." Gustus clenched his chest. "Avenge us, my son's son, last of my family. Be strong and merciless."

"How do you know about the babies?" Wardor asked desperately. "Tell me."

"Air is your enemy. I have a friend among the Elders who has told me that . . . ." Suddenly Gustus' eyes opened wide and his lips moved as if he were still talking, but no words came out of his mouth. He collapsed with a faint moan and died.

Wardor kneeled beside his grandfather. "Tell me," he cried, but there was no response. "Not one Wanderer or Rescue Flyer will survive once I am finished with them," Wardor said. "I promise." He lifted his right hand to his head in salute.

After a short moment of silence and grief, Wardor got up, lifted the body of his grandfather over his shoulder, and walked out of his dark, quiet fortress. Nobody observed Wardor spreading his wings and flying high into the air towards the mountains. He landed at the edge of the endless gorge and put his grandfather's body carefully down beside its rugged edge.

"Death Flyer," he yelled. "Accept this body and take it into your realm. I will avenge him." Wardor kneeled, kissed the cold cheeks of his last relative and pushed him over the edge. He got up resolutely, his mind filled with hatred and anger. "I will find those babies, no matter what. I will show the Flyers what has been going on for years. A conspiracy of the worst kind - the protection of Wanderers, our sworn enemy."

Wardor opened his wings and flew back to the War Flyers' headquarters where he commanded one lieutenant and twenty Flyers to follow him. They lined up in front of Wardor's fortress, which towered like a black monster into the dark sky. Wardor had selected his strongest, tallest warriors; in their black uniforms they looked threatening. They opened their wings and lifted up gracefully, but they were deadly, their long swords secured on their golden belts. The wind was in their favor and they reached the Mountain of Glory quickly. Before landing on the flat, quiet plateau beside the small creek, they soared above the stone library until Wardor gave the command to attack. They raced through the sky and landed like lightning.

Wardor marched toward the wooden door and kicked it open with a single kick.

"Search everywhere," he yelled. "Those who interfere or try to stop you, arrest them. Those who resist, kill them."

The Elders were rounded up quickly and brought into the large meeting hall. Two guards were killed and four others bound in chains. A Healing Flyer was dragged out of the basement and brutally pushed in front of the Elders. Two small beds were brought up and thrown into the hall.

"What is going on here, Wardor? Explain yourself. You and your thugs were not invited to enter these halls. This is treason," Air proclaimed.

"Treason?" Wardor laughed. "You are talking about treason? You are in collusion with the Wanderers and accuse me of treason because I'm uncovering the truth? I am declaring Walhalor, the state of emergency," Wardor shouted. "The Elders are no longer fit to make decisions. I, Wardor, Lord of the War Flyers, evoke the right to protect all Flyers."

"This is preposterous and you know it. How dare you," Earth protested.

"You should know that I have the right to do this. It is the law and I have the backing of my lieutenants. But then, what do you know about our laws? You have been breaking the most important one of all, the one that is the foundation of our community. Tell me where the babies are," Wardor demanded. He had drawn his sword and was pointing its tip against Air's chest.

"You are mistaken and foolish in your action," Air replied calmly. "I should have known you would take such drastic measures. I should have known you would be capable of this."

"Be quiet old Flyer and answer my question."

"Like I said, you are foolish. There are no babies here," Air repeated.

"He is right, my Lord. No sign of any baby," a War Flyer said.

Wardor turned violently and slashed his sword across the chest of the warrior who had spoken. The warrior yelled in pain and tumbled to the ground, blood gushing out of the deadly cut.

"Take this place apart," Wardor screamed. "Find me those babies. You four stay here and keep an eye on the prisoners," he continued, pointing at four warriors. "No one is allowed to leave or to enter. Do you hear me?"

"Yes, my Lord," the four warriors said in unison.

"You have made the biggest mistake of your life, Wardor," Air said, trying to gain control over his anger. His voice shook with fury. "You will pay for this."

Wardor looked at him with a smile and said, "Don't waste your breath on me, old man. You must realize your time is over. Your precious Rescue Flyers, especially Aldor, will be next, and you are unable to warn them." He smashed his fist into Air's face, turned around and walked out the door.

One of his lieutenants ran after him and asked, "What shall we do now, my Lord?"

"You are in charge here," Wardor replied. "I will return to our headquarters and inform the others. Where are your warriors?"

"Eight inside the library looking for the babies, four in the hall with the prisoners, and seven on the plateau, my Lord."

"Well done. No one enters the library. Have your warriors well positioned around the plateau. Kill anyone who is not a War Flyer and who tries to approach the mountain. Understood?"

"Yes, my Lord."

Wardor opened his wings and flew back to his mountain. There he rang the alarm bell and his lieutenants assembled in the war hall within minutes. Wardor laid out his plan. At last he could move forward with this plan he had been working on for the past two months.

Now is my time. I can feel it, he thought. He was overwhelmed with hatred and anger.

"I will put an end to the Wanderers and the Rescue Flyers," he bellowed, and his lieutenants listened. "By tomorrow evening I will be in control of all the Flyers, and I will control all the mountains. War has begun and nothing or no one will stop me." He turned to his lieutenants and yelled, "Who is with me?"

"You have our lives and our commitment, Lord Wardor," his lieutenants yelled in unison.

"So it is said, so it is done," he replied, laughing loudly.

CHAPTER NINE
The Truth

"Please sit down," Aldor said. They had entered a small cottage on the training grounds on the Mountain of Sun. "What I have to tell you will surprise you, maybe even shock you, but the alliance has decided to invite you two to join us."

Timo and Val looked at each other in confusion. They trusted Aldor completely, but they had never heard of the alliance before.

"What is the alliance?" Timo asked.

"It started six years ago," Aldor began. "A Flyer gave birth to a Wanderer, one without wings. She was born in the Halls of Healing, and Dodor, Lord of the Healing Flyers, brought her to the Elders. He knew about the Law of Return and didn't know what to do."

Val listened intently and thought about her brother. Her previous vision of him returned, but this time he was being thrown down the Cliff.

"This is what has happened to your brother, Val," Aldor explained. "He is a Wanderer."

"Yes, he is," Val replied angrily, "and I love him, no matter what." She stood up angrily and continued, "I can even sense him. We have the same blood. You will not get him."

"Calm down, Val," Aldor said gently. "I am on your side."

Timo looked from Val to Aldor and back to Val, he didn't understand.

"You took my brother away to kill him, to satisfy that stupid law," Val protested.

"No, we took your brother away to protect him, to save him from Wardor and his men. We, the alliance, wouldn't allow any baby to be killed, no matter what the laws say. We believe in the one people, Flyers and Wanderers together, one family."

"But that is treason," Val replied.

"Yes, we understand that, and one day we will have to stand trial for it, but in the meantime we do what we think is the right thing to do. The laws were made in the past and who knows why they were made. As long as I live, no baby will be given to the wind."

He looked at Val and saw she believed him. Val felt awkward and worried when she looked at Aldor. *I was wrong,* she thought.

"I am happy you feel and think about your brother this way. It is the same way the Elders and the alliance think about the Wanderers. The old writings talk about a time when there was only one people, not two, Flyers and Wanderers together, no difference and no segregation, no hatred between us, and no war. We were one, united in trust and connected in blood." Aldor looked at Timo and Val to see if he could detect their reactions to what he had just said. "What do you think, Timo?" he asked suddenly.

"For now I'm listening with an open mind, but you know what pains my heart. The Wanderers killed my father."

"Yes, Timo. I know your pain, it is also my pain, but no one knows if the Wanderers killed Gildor. He was killed by an arrow in the back, an arrow that bore the markings of the War Flyers."

Timo listened quietly, but tears of anger and hatred filled his eyes. He pulled his hand into a fist and his heart beat faster. Through his clenched teeth he hissed, "Wardor."

"No one knows," Aldor said, "but I kept the arrow and I will find out who released it and who killed Gildor." Aldor rose, walked over to Timo and put his hand on Timo's shoulder. "Let me continue, please, and listen closely. After I

finish what I have to say, I will ask you an important question."
Aldor returned to his chair, sat down, and continued.

"The alliance is a group of Flyers who don't believe in the
Law of Return and who cannot justify killing babies. We
believe that the Wanderers and the Flyers are one people. We
decided to contact the Wanderers and entrust them with the
Wanderer babies born in the Mountains, to allow them to raise
them. To our surprise, we discovered that some Wanderers had
given birth to Flyers, but their leaders had killed them. The
Wanderers we found share our beliefs that we are one people.
However, many others still believe in the war."

"But contacting the Wanderers is also treason," Val said.

"Yes and we are fully aware of this, but our consciences
and our moral values wouldn't allow us to follow through with
a law that kills innocent babies. We tried to have that law
abolished in the Council meetings, but Wardor opposed it. His
ancestors were the ones who drafted the Law of Return. He
also knows of another law, one that gives the lord of the War
Flyers the right to evoke a state of emergency, the so-called
Walhalor. In case of suspected treason by the Elders, the lord
of the War Flyers can take control of the mountains. He
becomes the law."

"Impossible," Val said, outraged.

"The alliance has been walking a fine line, but we believe
that Wardor suspects something. You have forced our hand,
Val, by finding your brother. Your discovery proves that we
are one people."

"What were you planning to do with my brother?"

"Dodor left last night with one baby and two Healing
Flyers to meet with the Wanderers."

"Why?" asked Val.

"You know what Wardor would do with your brother if he
found him. We had to act quickly, especially after the last

Council meeting that determined Timo's penalty. Wardor was livid and upset about our decision. It may have pushed him over the edge. He is probably looking for revenge. He has already threatened the Elders. Every day he is becoming bolder with his accusations. Who knows exactly what he is capable of?"

"So what do we do now?" Val asked anxiously.

"I have to know if you trust me."

"I do trust you, now I trust you completely," Val replied immediately.

"Then you know what you have to do, don't you?"

"Yes, I do, but can you forgive me?"

Timo stood up abruptly and said, "Stop. What do you have to do, Val?"

"What about you, Timo?" Aldor asked, ignoring Timo's question. "Do you trust me?"

"Yes, Aldor. I trust you like my father trusted you."

"Good. Now tell Timo what you did last night, Val."

*** *** ***

Val closed her eyes and the memories of the previous night came alive in front of her. She watched Timo lift off the plateau in front of the Halls of Healing. She waited in the shadow of the old oak tree until he was well on his way to the Mountain of Clouds to meet with the Council. The weather was perfect for a rescue. The wind was calm and the moon was hiding behind heavy clouds, the harbingers of the coming storm season. She was wearing her black flight clothing and carrying a harness. Crouching in the shadow a few more minutes, Val carefully observed her surroundings and the sky to make sure nobody could see her. She knew much attention was on the Mountain of Clouds that evening with all the Elders and Lords discussing Timo's punishment. This was her chance.

"Everything is quiet," she whispered. "I am ready," she said to encourage herself. "Brother, I am coming."

She quickly ran across the plateau, opened her wings and lifted into the sky. "Off to the Mountain of Glory again?" the wind asked.

"How did you know?" Val replied, shocked.

"I have been watching you, you know, I am always here. I saw them carrying your brother to the mountain. What are you up to?"

"Have you told anybody?"

"You should know better. I can only talk to you about matters that concern you. I can't tell you what Wardor is up to."

"What is he up to? Please tell me," Val pleaded, but the wind only hissed and howled.

After reaching the plateau in front of the library she ran toward the old building while hiding in its shadow. Everything was calm and quiet. She looked at the sky again and waited. Nothing moved. She took the same way into the building she had taken the previous night, quietly opening the door that led into the basement. She sneaked down the rocky steps without making a sound. The two babies were sleeping in their beds; nobody else was in the room. She rushed over to her brother, picked him up gently and gave him a quick kiss. A little startled, he opened his eyes and was about to cry when Val whispered into his ear, "It is me, your sister. I am here to rescue you. Don't cry, little one. Be strong." The tiny baby squeaked a couple of times then settled down as if he had understood his sister. Val carefully put him into her harness, turned around and rushed up the cold stairs. At the top she waited and listened, no noise, no sounds, just silence except for her heartbeat. She opened the door and ran through the hallways. When she reached the front door she pressed down the door handle, pushed open the door and rushed out to the plateau. She hid in the shadow of the library while she studied the sky, nothing. She ran across the plateau, jumped off the cliff and opened her wings. The wind picked her up gently and helped her to gain speed. She soared higher and higher until the clouds swallowed her, then she turned east towards the Mountain of Wind.

*** *** ***

"You took your brother out of the library?" Timo asked surprised. "Why didn't you tell me about your plan?"

"I wanted to," Val objected, "but you'd already made up your mind to go to the Council meeting."

"And that was a wise decision," Aldor interjected. "If he hadn't come, he would have lost his right to fly. I wouldn't have been able to prevent his wings from being clipped. Where is the baby?"

"I brought him to my grandmother's place. Her small cottage stands near the old forest on the East Side of the large meadow on the Mountain of Wind," Val explained.

"Your brother is not safe!" Aldor exclaimed.

"I trust my grandmother. She understands," Val protested.

"That's not what I mean. If Wardor finds your brother we can't save him. Wardor's army is too strong, the Rescue Flyers are outnumbered."

"Your plan for my brother was best," said Val, "and I thank you for that. But what do I do now?"

"It is so important for you to know the truth now. I will tell you the names of the other Rescue Flyers who are part of the alliance. They are our three Elders: Air, Wind, and Earth, as well as Dodor, Wolf, the Golden Eagle, and all the Rescue Flyers."

"Honor and loyalty," Timo said.

"Honor and loyalty," Val said.

"We will have to go get your brother and bring him to the Wanderers. There is no other way."

"I can show you how to get there," Val said.

"Good, let's go then. Timo, are you ready?"

"Always," Timo replied.

The three Flyers stood close together and shook hands. A large burden fell from Val's shoulders; she knew now what had happened, and she knew now whom she could trust.

Suddenly the door to the cottage was pushed open violently and an exhausted Rescue Flyer rushed in. "It has happened, Aldor, my Lord," he bellowed. "Wardor has declared Walhalor. The Elders are under arrest and the War Flyers are on the hunt. They have occupied the Mountain of Glory, the Mountain of Life, the Mountain of Wind and the Mountain of Clouds. They are on their way here, to the Mountain of Sun."

Aldor rushed to the Flyer and placed his hand on his right shoulder.

"You know what you have to do," Aldor said. "We will meet at the ancient hiding place called Ardar, deep in the Old Mountains. Go and warn as many as you can, my friend. Honor and loyalty to you."

"Honor and loyalty, my Lord," the Rescue Flyer replied, and was gone.

"Val, you know how to reach Ardar. You and Timo must go get Dino. We need his talent for calculating the wind and the weather. He is a navigator, but doesn't know yet about his gift. Tell him to bring the four books, he will know which ones I mean. I will see you tonight. Be safe. Honor and loyalty."

"What about my brother?" Val said in alarm.

"He will be safer where he is now than with us," Aldor said. "We can't care for a baby if we are on the run. I will send word to Wolf. He will find a way to watch over your brother. He will inform us if he is in any danger. Now go. Time is pressing."

"Honor and loyalty, Aldor," Val and Timo said together.

Aldor looked at Timo and Val quickly and laid his hands on their shoulders.

"The time has come, sooner than I would have liked it to. Believe in your gift and trust your instinct. The wind is your friend. Take care, Val and Timo. You have the gift, listen to it and believe in yourselves. Honor and loyalty."

The three ran out of the cottage and lifted up into the air right away. Aldor turned towards the Mountain of Glory, and Timo and Val flew to the Mountain of Wind.

"How will we convince Dino to come with us?" Val asked.

"I know how. Let's hurry," Timo replied.

They moved their wings faster until they reached their desired height just above a fine layer of clouds, then folded their wings close to their bodies and shot through the air like a hunting hayabusa in a nose dive, determined to catch its spotted prey on the ground.

CHAPTER TEN

Walhalor

Wardor was quick to organize his War Flyers. He informed his lieutenants that the execution of his plan was to begin first thing in the morning. The War Flyers were to take control of the Five Mountains. The lords of the other Flyer groups were to be arrested and brought to the Mountain of Glory where they would be held together with the Elders. All Rescue Flyers were to be hunted down, put in chains, and brought to the dungeons of Wardor's headquarters.

The War Flyers were fast and efficient. By the time the sun disappeared behind the mountains in the west, they had conquered the remaining four mountains. Wardor flew to the Mountain of Glory to meet with his lieutenants.

"I am in control now," he proclaimed as soon as he had entered the meeting hall in the stone library.

"How dare . . . ," Stodor, Lord of the Storm Flyers, tried to protest but was hit in the face by one of the War Flyers

"Quiet, you fool. No one has allowed you to speak."

"Thank you," Wardor said and gave his warrior an approving smile. "Let me see who is here. I heard Stodor, I see Raidor, Air, Wind, Earth . . . ." Wardor's face turned red and the veins on the side of his head popped up. "Where are the others?" he yelled, spit flying out of his mouth. "Where are those traitors Aldor and Dodor? Where are Wolf and the Golden Eagle?"

"We didn't find them, my Lord," one of the first-ranking lieutenants said. "But we found out that Dodor left the Mountains last night. He was seen flying towards the Flatlands."

"What about the Rescue Flyers?" Wardor hissed.

"We have captured forty. The rest have escaped. They have been put in chains and are sitting in the dungeons awaiting your arrival, my Lord. Your servants are ready to torture them if they are unwilling to answer your questions freely."

"Only forty? There should have been at least sixty. What about the Mountains?" Wardor asked impatiently.

"They are under your command, my Lord. There was no resistance on the Mountain of Wind. At least thirty War Flyers are stationed on each mountain. The Storm Flyers, the Healing Flyers, the Rain Flyers, and all the non-assigned Flyers are waiting for you on the Mountain of Wind, in the Meadow of Celebration. They are eager to hear your word, my Lord."

"Well done, Lieutenant. So, Aldor is on the run without support and without hope. Good, very good. I'm not worried about twenty or so Rescue Flyers. Once I have talked to the Flyers on the Mountain of Wind, everyone will be hunting Aldor and his doomed Rescue Flyers. Aldor will be dead, soon."

"He is probably hiding at Ardar," one lieutenant suggested.

"Don't be a fool. Ardar is a myth. It doesn't exist. Has anyone ever seen it? No! Aldor is flying around aimlessly with nowhere to go and nowhere to hide. I control the Mountains now, and no one will escape me." Wardor looked pleased, his initial anger gone. He slowly walked past his prisoners and looked at them with disgust. He stopped in front of Air and said, "I have warned you, old Flyer, but no. Your arrogance and disrespect blinded and deceived you."

Air didn't respond. He was glad that the alliance had escaped. He didn't worry about himself or the other Elders beside him. They were ready for what was to come. They had prepared for this moment. He knew that with Aldor being free Timo and Val would be free as well. The future was now in the hands of the young ones; with the guidance of the lord of the Rescue Flyers they would be taught well. *Wardor, you fool*, he thought. *This is the beginning of your end and the end of the War Flyers.*

"Watch these traitors," Wardor commanded. "My people are waiting for me and I don't want to disappoint them." He spat on the ground in front of the prisoners then turned his back on them. Once on the mountain plateau, he opened his massive wings and flew to the Mountain of Wind. Three of his lieutenants followed.

I did it, Wardor thought as he soared above the clouds. *My revenge will be merciless.*

*** *** ***

"Down there," Timo called as he raced towards the ground.

Val followed, impressed with Timo's flight and maneuvers. She had a difficult time keeping up. *He knows so much about flying without any training*, she thought. *He is the best at flying I have ever seen. Side rolls, wind loops, downdraft anticipation, nosedives, angle slides, horizontal sailing, ridge flying. How does he know all that?*

Timo landed in Dino's backyard. He ran toward the back door. He quickly opened it and quietly sneaked through the house and up the stairs toward Dino's room. Val followed him like a shadow, quickly and silently. Timo knew the house well. He had spent many rainy afternoons and many cold winter days here with Dino and his family.

Without hesitation, Timo pushed Dino's door open and walked to the middle of his room. Val was right beside him. Before Dino could realize what was happening, Timo warned, "Don't say a word. Just listen. We don't have much time. Take your four most important books and follow us. Wardor has declared Walhalor and is taking control of the Mountains. We must fly to Ardar."

"Ar . . . Ardar," Dino stuttered. "The legendary birth place of the first Rescue Flyer who had the gift. The mystical place where the golden eagles live and soar. The dark place where the Flyer of Death rules. Nobody can reach that place even if it exists."

"Val knows where it is. Now hurry. The War Flyers are on their way."

"Val? How would she know?" Dino protested. Spotting Val behind Timo he continued sheepishly, "Oh, hi Val. How are you doing?"

"Hi, Dino," Val replied.

"Never mind, Dino," interrupted Timo. "Just trust me and come."

Dino continued talking nervously while gathering up his books. "I read that Ardar is impossible to reach." The first book he picked up was *Soaring*, written by Gildor, Timo's father. He looked at it briefly before putting it in his backpack. "One has to fly through hurricanes and whirlwinds, through vertical drafts and horizontal storm cells, through unstable atmospheres and thunderstorms, through squall lines and clouds of crystal ice. No, thank you. I think I will take my chances with Wardor." Dino was holding *Severe Storm Structures: Forward Flank and Rear Flank Downdrafts*, written by Air.

"I need you, Dino. And Aldor asked me to get you," Timo insisted.

Picking up *Cloud Lines and Rising Air*, written by Wind, Dino began to hurry. "Aldor? Aldor asked for me by name?" Dino asked proudly. *He knows my name!* he thought. Forgotten were his worries and concerns about Ardar and how to get there.

"Yes," Timo said. "Aldor knows your name."

"But I am grounded," Dino remembered while picking up the last book he would take with him, *The Art of Falling*, written by Earth. Dino looked at the cover and recited from the book by heart:

We can fly and we can soar. We can travel along the trade winds and the sea breeze. We can marvel at the world below us and rise above the mountain on a sine wave. But never forget that we can also fall. The earth will always have us back, because no one can stay with the clouds forever.

The three friends looked at each other and suddenly realized that the wind of life had caught up with them and surrounded them.

"Wardor is going to take control," Timo explained, determined to get going. "Air said that we are the future. I don't know what he meant by it, but I will find out. We have to be ready for whatever lies ahead of us. I will not allow War Flyers to justify killing innocent people because of old, outdated and cruel laws. Let's hurry, Dino. Time is running out. The War Flyers are on their way." Timo grabbed Dino's hand and pulled him through the door, down the stairs, and out into the backyard. Val took the backpack full of books and swung it over her shoulders. She joined the other two who stood frozen, staring into the sky.

"War Flyers," Timo hissed. "Up there in the sky." Timo pointed. "It really has started." The War Flyers were flying above them in an X formation. The three friends watched as the

War Flyers split up and flew in four different directions, ready to land and fight whomever tried to resist them.

"To the Cliff," Val said. "Quickly."

The three loped along the edge of the main street below the big trees, along the nicely arranged gardens of their neighbors, up along the field road, and into the old forest towards the Cliff. For Timo and Dino it was almost like déjà vu. They had taken the same route just four days before. They stopped briefly at the edge of the Cliff and looked at one other.

"I have seen this place in my vision," Val said, looking worried. "They held my brother over this cliff, then threw him into the abyss."

"What you saw will not happen. Your brother will be safe," Timo reassured her.

As if they'd known what they were going to do, Timo grabbed Dino's right hand and Val took Dino's left hand. Both jumped off the Cliff at the same time, dragging a screaming Dino behind them.

*** *** ***

A nervous crowd had gathered at the Meadow of Celebration on the Mountain of Wind. The meadow was a circular grassy area located between the four villages of the Mountain of Wind. Several War Flyers were positioned at strategic locations, surrounding the crowd. Frantic chatter and angry questions filled the air. The place sounded like a disrupted beehive. Suddenly, everyone became quiet; Wardor had arrived. He floated silently from the sky, followed by his lieutenants. He wore the black war uniform of the lord of the War Flyers. The golden embroidery on his cloak shimmered in the evening sun and Wardor looked impressive with his bow and arrows slung across his back and his long, heavy sword hanging from his right side. He landed on a small podium that had been hastily built for him.

"Welcome, my brothers and sisters, people of the Flyers, my people," Wardor began. "I have sad news for you. This is a dark day in our history, but don't be alarmed. Everyone is safe, and the situation is under control. Last night I arrested the Elders and declared Walhalor." He paused strategically to see how the crowd would react.

A roar went through the Flyers. Some Flyers began to cry, while other stood in shock. Others yelled words that were swallowed by the noise that rose from the upset crowd. Wardor lifted his arms and the Flyers became quiet again, like an easily controllable mob.

"We have discovered treason, treason by those we trusted most. Our Elders! Our Elders — Earth, Wind, and Air — have been in contact with the Wanderers, our most hated enemies. They have forged hidden plans and broken our oldest, most valued laws. I've had them arrested. However, their accomplices, Dodor and Aldor, have escaped. Dodor is on the run. He was last seen flying towards the Flatlands. Aldor, our most trusted Flyer and Lord of the Rescue Flyers, is in hiding."

"That is impossible," yelled one of the Flyers in the crowd.

"These are all lies. The Elders would never betray us," another voice cried out.

Wardor waited. He was hoping the crowd would grow angrier. It did.

"Aldor is honorable and just," someone yelled.

"It can't be. You are a liar, Wardor."

"This is outrageous. This is a plot designed so you can take control."

The shouts became louder and the accusations became bolder and more aggressive. The crowd moved closer to Wardor. *This is working too well*, Wardor thought. It was time to speak again. He had the Flyers right where he wanted them. The crowd was truly vulnerable when he raised his arms again. They were emotional, acting without thinking.

"I'm here in person, to talk to you, my people," he yelled. "I am not hiding or sending only messengers. I am here with you on this dark day so I can hear your concerns and answer your questions. I am listening to you. Before you judge, let me tell you why I am here."

The crowd became quiet and began to listen. Wardor's timing had been perfect.

"As I said, the Elders are in contact with our sworn enemy, the Wanderers, those barbarians who have killed our ancestors, massacred our families, destroyed our homes, and who only recently killed our greatest Flyer ever, Gildor. The Elders have hidden the truth from all of us for many years now." He waited a few seconds then proclaimed, "Wanderers have been born among us."

The crowd went silent. There wasn't a whisper. All stood in shock.

"Wanderers have been born in the Mountains by some of our Flyers. Those babies were taken to our enemies by the Rescue Flyers so they could grow up and train as warriors to kill us eventually. I know of at least six babies who were born wingless. Here are the names of the families who were informed their babies were stillborn." Wardor called out the family names. "Am I right? Were you told that your babies are dead?"

The named families confirmed what Wardor was telling them.

"Treason," one Flyer yelled. "The Elders have betrayed us."

"We are doomed," another wailed.

Wardor smiled to himself. He couldn't believe how easy it was to control and manipulate this emotional crowd. "Wait!" Wardor raised his arms. "There is more." Wardor moved forward, closer to the listening Flyers.

"I am one of you. My family and ancestors have died to keep you safe, and I will do the same. I will protect you, but you must support me. Aldor killed Gildor to gain control of the lordship of the Rescue Flyers, and those savages, the Wanderers, helped him."

The crowd became angry again.

"I believe that Aldor has kidnapped Timo, Gildor's only son and true Lord of the Rescue Flyers. He plans to kill him. We have to stop him and prepare for war against the Wanderers who will come to destroy us. Who is with me?" Wardor bellowed. "Who is with me and supports Walhalor?"

The crowd cheered wildly.

"We will follow you wherever you lead us, Wardor," the crowd yelled.

"Who is with me?" he repeated.

"We are. We are." Cheers went through the crowd in an ever-growing wave. "Wardor, Wardor, Wardor," the crowd began to chant.

"So it is done," Wardor whispered. He listened to his name and felt pleased with himself.

"So it is said, so it is done," he yelled. "Follow and join me. War it will be. This is what I say and what I decide. Let this be written in the Book of Statements."

CHAPTER ELEVEN

Ardar

Dino's throat hurt from all his screaming, but he'd eventually found enough courage to fly by himself. He was following Val with Timo right behind him. They flew high in the sky above a thick layer of clouds heading north into the Old Mountain range, towards Ardar. Many stories existed about that mysterious, legendary place, but no one had ever seen it. The stories were filled with violence, anger, and death: those who entered Ardar uninvited found a brutal ending. Huge, ugly creatures controlled the sky, and three-legged beasts roamed the ground. These stories were told to children who didn't behave, to scare them. "If you don't behave, we will send you to Ardar where the eagles will eat you alive," or "If you don't behave, the Death Flyer will come from Ardar and take you." Dino remembered the long nights of his childhood, filled with fear and fright, and when he did finally fall asleep, his dreams were terrorized by the Death Flyer and by eagles with sharp claws. His parents had told him these terrifying stories many times!

Val, Timo, and Dino had been flying for several hours when Val suddenly turned right and folded her wings. She went into a nosedive.

Everything will be fine, Dino thought, horrified. *Timo will rescue me.*

The air was getting slowly warmer as they penetrated through the clouds, and the mountains became visible again. Dino was overwhelmed by what he saw. Green valleys, steep, snow-covered mountain peaks, and roaring waterfalls lay below. Yellow and red flowers covered the ground, birds sang, and mountain goats climbed the steep cliffs with their young ones behind them. Val was flying very quickly, holding Dino's hand so he wouldn't fall behind. Timo was close behind them. They maneuvered through tight canyons, along rugged mountain edges, above huge treetops, and down steep cliffs. Val flew over the edge of another cliff and raced headfirst toward a silvery blue pool that formed at the foot of a foaming waterfall. Suddenly she opened her wings and stopped in mid-air. Dino, unable to open his wings as quickly, flew past her towards the water. Timo went into a nosedive and grabbed Dino's ankles when he reached him. Timo opened his wings. As the oncoming rush of air pushed his wings backward, Timo screamed with pain. Dino put his hands in front of his face and screamed as well, but Timo was able to slow their fall until they were hovering in the air. Dino dangled from Timo's hands, the top of his head touching the icy water; he had an instant headache, like a brain freeze when drinking cold water too fast on a hot summer day. Dino had stopped screaming. Timo turned Dino around and flew them both up to where Val was waiting.

"Too fast, Val," Timo protested. "Dino can't fly as fast as we can."

"I'm sorry," said Val while looking at Dino who was as white as a dove. "We're here," she added encouragingly. She pointed at a crack in the cliff, flew towards it and landed on a narrow ledge. She folded her wings, turned sideways, and disappeared through the tiny opening in the grey rock face. Dino and Timo followed. Once inside the opening, the three stared into a huge cave that was barely lit, though many brightly burning torches were fastened into the rugged, stone walls. Two Rescue Flyers approached and greeted them. They had bows and arrows slung over their shoulders and long swords in their hands.

Rescue Flyers with weapons, Timo thought. *There is so much I don't know.*

"Follow us," one of the Flyers instructed.

They walked several hundred meters down into the cave along a small path at the edge of a steep wall until they reached a huge plateau from which many different paths led deeper into the darkness. Torches hung all around, their flames reflected in the green crystals that made up the surrounding walls. Green beams of light crisscrossed everywhere.

Several Rescue Flyers had gathered in the center of the plateau, and in their midst stood Aldor. By his side was the huge Golden Eagle.

"Welcome," Aldor said when he became aware of the young Flyers. All eyes focused on them. "We have been waiting for you." He introduced them to the Rescue Flyers. "This is Val, whom you already know from the Mountain of Sun. Beside her is Timo, an excellent, talented, and smart Flyer who has the gift and who is also Gildor's son. The third is Dino, navigator extraordinaire. I hope you brought your books?"

Dino blushed and stuttered a quiet, "Yes."

"Good. These are our remaining Rescue Flyers. The others were captured and arrested by Wardor's army. May I introduce the Golden Eagle, member of the Council and protector of the Mountain of Clouds?"

The three friends bowed deeply to him.

"You did well bringing our new friends to us safely, Val. Thank you," Aldor said, smiling at Val. Val smiled back. Aldor stepped closer to her and said, "I talked to Wolf. He will send five of his best trackers to where your brother is in hiding. For now, your brother is safe. If anything changes, you will be immediately informed."

"Thank you, Aldor," Val replied, feeling a little relieved. She had been so worried and was still angry with herself for what she had done. She had taken her brother from a safe place into danger instead of rescuing him.

"Now, please join us," said Aldor and turned back to the others. "We are outlaws now. Wardor has taken control of the Five Mountains and has united the remaining Flyers under him. The Elders and the rest of the Council are under arrest and charged with treason. Everyone is allowed to hunt and kill me. I am charged with the murder of Gildor. Wardor has declared Walhalor." Everyone was quiet, listening in disbelief. "The good news is that no one has lost his life. I have sent two Rescue Flyers to warn Dodor and the Wanderers who are in alliance with us. War is upon us."

"What can we do, Aldor?" One of the Flyers asked.

"There are four books. Within their pages lies a plan hidden in the words and the stories told, a plan to overcome Walhalor. These books are named *Soaring, Severe Storm Structures, Forward Flank and Back Flank Downdrafts*, and *The Art of Falling*."

"I have read those books and have brought them with me," Dino said excitedly.

"Good, that is why I asked for you to come. The plan within those books can only be discovered by a navigator like you, Dino."

Dino blushed again. "Me?"

"Yes, you, Dino." Aldor smiled. "Your family comes from a long line of one of the best navigators. Fourteen years ago, something special happened. Three baby Flyers were born under the strangest circumstances. The moon and the North Star were in perfect alignment when the three of you were born, and from that moment we knew the three of you were special. All the talent of your families has been pooled within you. Dino, you are a great navigator with innate instincts and a keen sense for minute details. Val, you are a great Flyer with foresight and the ability to envision the future, skills that you will soon develop fully. Timo, you have the gift. You can sense the wind, and you can even communicate with it. You can taste the air and sense the atmosphere. You will be the greatest Flyer ever. The future lies in your hands.

"These are great talents but also great burdens. I hope you will accept them as a special gift given to you by the ancient Flyers. The three of you hold the combined knowledge and talent of all the ancient Flyers."

Everyone was quiet. Timo, Dino, and Val looked briefly at one other. They had sensed that they were unlike other young Flyers but had never imagined they were as different as Aldor had just described.

"But I am not a navigator," Dino suddenly said, realizing the importance of Aldor's explanation. "One day, yes, I am hoping to be one, but I am just your average Flyer who . . . ."

"Who knows the four books better than anyone else," Aldor said, finishing Dino's sentence. "I have read your dissertation on *The Art of Falling*. It is very impressive and contains insight that only a true navigator could have. Your paper will be added to the Book of Statements, Dino, so future generations can read it and learn from it. Your friend Timo trusted you with your calculations when he jumped off the Cliff. Remember?

"Think about it for a while. All three of you."

In his heart Timo heard all the songs the wind had sung to him. He remembered all the moments he had spent flying, sensing the air and feeling the temperature, always accompanied by the wind. He knew that Aldor was right. He had known for a long time, but he hadn't quite understood what he'd been experiencing. He'd thought he had to prove himself to his father, but all along he'd been his father's son — strong and committed, dependable and resourceful, cautious and adventurous.

At first Val didn't know what Aldor was talking about, then she remembered her visions. In the past she'd thought she was daydreaming or that her mind had been playing tricks on her. The more she thought about it now, the more frightened she became. *If Aldor is right, and I can really see the future, then my brother will die,* she thought. Her hands were trembling. *And what about the visions I had about Timo?*

Dino accepted Aldor's words as he heard them. He was proud of what he was hearing and completely committed. He had read about the ancient navigators, how they had found a way to fly through the passages of the Old Mountains and had found the Five Mountains. *Yes,* he thought. *I will be the greatest navigator.* His face was glowing with excitement.

"Accept your gifts and learn how to use them," Aldor's voice echoed through the cave. "Think about it while you rest. Tomorrow, Timo will begin his training and Val will accompany him. Dino will sit with the Golden Eagle and together they will review the four books. The Golden Eagle will tell you about our history and values. With these, Dino, you might find some connections within the books. I hope that by tomorrow evening Dodor will be back, then you, Val, can talk to him about your visions. He will help you to understand what you see."

Val looked into Aldor's eyes and gave him a brave smile, despite her concerns and fear.

Aldor looked into the worried eyes of the three young Flyers who stood in front of him. "I understand this is coming soon, too soon," he added. "I was hoping to have more time with you, to guide you and to carefully move you toward your destiny. The situation has changed so dramatically and so quickly that you will have to accept immediately who and what you are. I ask a lot from you, but I have no choice."

"I am honored by your trust, Aldor," said Dino, mighty proud of what Aldor had said about him. "I will find the connections and we will all return to our mountains. We can't allow Wardor to succeed with his warmongering."

"Well said, my friend," Aldor replied. "Now get some rest."

*** *** ***

The night passed quickly and Timo, Val, and Dino were up early. After breakfast with all the other Flyers, Aldor held a quick meeting before the day began.

"Good morning," Aldor greeted everyone. "A busy day lies ahead of us. Eagle and Dino will go to the Cave of Vision and start searching for the hidden clues in the four books."

"Why are the clues hidden? Why wasn't the plan communicated directly?" asked Timo. "Didn't the three Elders and my father trust anyone?"

"The three Elders and your father, Timo, trusted us, but no one knows how the future might develop. Your father was killed, I could have been killed, or the three Elders could have been killed. The plan could have fallen into the wrong hands. That is why it was hidden. The plan can only be found by someone who has honor and loyalty, someone who is true to his friends and family, someone like you three young ones."

Aldor paused for a while to let his words echo from the walls and sink into the minds of everyone who was listening.

"Now, Dino, go with Eagle and think wisely. Take your time, but remember that war is upon us.

"Val, collect your weapons and continue with your training with the Rescue Flyers. They will teach you well. Listen to their instructions and follow their guidance.

"Timo, come with me. You have much to learn and only a little time."

All went their way. Aldor and Timo were alone in the large cave.

"Here is where it all began," Aldor explained. "The history of the Rescue Flyers started here in this cave when a young, pregnant female Flyer became lost in the mountains during a wild thunderstorm. She found refuge here and gave birth. The baby Flyer was the first one born with the gift. He could talk to the wind, taste the air, and feel the atmosphere. All Rescue Flyers are related to that baby, which makes us all family. That is why the bond among us is strong and our loyalty committed. It is also why our honor is complete and inclusive. Nothing can break the bond of blood."

The two went to the small crack in the cliff and stepped out into a bright morning.

"You have the gift and it is stronger in you than in anyone else. Your destiny is to become the next Lord of the Rescue Flyers. The lordship is usually passed on from father to son, so when you are ready to take on the responsibility to lead us, and you know when that will be, tell me and I will step aside."

"Why would you do that, Aldor?"

"Honor and loyalty. I do not want to hold onto something that is not mine. Your father is my best friend, which makes you my godchild."

They looked at each other for a long time. Aldor recalled some painful experiences he had tried to hide as well as he could. He remembered his wife and his son who had been lost to the cold downdraft. With sad eyes he looked at Timo and saw a slight resemblance to his missing son.

"Now," Aldor finally said, "for your first lesson. Follow me and we will fly together. You must first learn patience. I will guide you." The two stepped out onto the small ledge, opened their wings, and dove into the depths. The wind found them immediately and quickly lifted them high above the mountains.

"Feel the wind, listen to it, and try to understand it. You know so much and feel it so strongly, but you have to learn how to connect your knowledge and senses. Neither is anything without the other."

Timo listened and knew what Aldor was talking about, but he didn't want to tell him that the wind had been talking to him for many years and that they were close friends already. Timo had realized his gift and had accepted it right from the beginning. Aldor was certainly right about Timo's impatience, though. The wind surrounded Timo tightly and Timo listened to its songs. Timo knew how to soar. He felt his senses and his muscles as they adjusted quickly to the changing atmosphere.

"Listen, feel, and know," Aldor said, gliding masterfully beside him. "Listen to the wind. It will always be with you. It is your friend."

I know, Timo thought. *The wind has sung lullabies to me for as long as I can remember.*

CHAPTER TWELVE

Dodor

Dodor lifted into the air, relieved that the Council meeting was over and glad that Timo's punishment wasn't too harsh. He didn't like Wardor very much and tried to avoid him as much as possible. He was returning to the Mountain of Glory to complete what had been discussed with the Elders. Dodor flew quietly and swiftly through the cold night. He was accompanied by two of his most trusted Healing Flyers. When they reached the old historic library, panic had erupted in the usually tranquil building. All the candles were lit, the guards were running around hectically, and the Healing Flyer who was watching over the babies was crying hysterically.

"What happened?" Dodor asked as he entered through the wide open door, addressing the first guard who crossed his path.

"One of the babies is gone."

"How is this possible? Nobody is allowed into these halls without being invited. Don't the old laws mean anything anymore?" As soon as he had said those words he realized what he had said. *We are breaking the old laws,* he thought. *We who are supposed to uphold them, we the Elders and most trusted Flyers.*

"We believe it was the spy who was here the previous night," explained the guard, interrupting Dodor's thoughts.

"Val," Dodor whispered under his breath. Aldor had told him who he suspected was the spy. *Val,* he thought. *What have you done?*

"We have to bring the other baby to safety," Dodor said to the Flyer. "Where is she?"

"Downstairs, sleeping," the guard replied.

Dodor and the two Healing Flyers ran through the hallways and down into the basement. As the guard had said, the baby was sleeping in her bed. Dodor lifted her up gently and wrapped her in a warm, soft blanket. He strapped on a harness and placed the baby carefully in it, holding her closely as if she were his own. The baby opened her eyes and looked at him with big, blue, questioning eyes.

"You will be safe, little one," Dodor whispered into small ears. "Everything will be fine."

He raced back up the stairs and through the brightly lit hallways. He jumped through the doorway followed closely by the two Healing Flyers. They took to the air immediately.

Large shadows approached from the West.

"War Flyers," he said to his companions. "Let's hurry."

He closed his wings slightly so he would fly faster. The night air blew across his face. He tucked the blanket tighter around the baby and with worried eyes looked down at the little girl who had fallen asleep again.

"Dark times lie ahead, my little Wanderer," he whispered softly.

They flew half the night until they spotted a signal fire burning low within the old, dead forest at the outskirts of the Flatlands. When they landed, three Wanderers greeted them happily, two women and a muscular man who was as tall as a bear and carrying a long, heavy sword.

"How was the flight, Dodor?" one of the women asked. She was blind and walked with the help of a cane. The Wanderers referred to her as Mot.

"I think Wardor has discovered the alliance and our mission. Just after I left, I saw several War Flyers approaching the Mountain of Glory. That can mean only one thing, Wardor is declaring Walhalor. Here, please take the baby."

Dodor carefully loosened the harness and gently handed over the sleeping baby to the second woman.

"Thank you," she said. "Where is the other baby?"

"He was taken," Dodor replied sadly.

"Taken? By whom?" Mot asked.

"We believe that his sister took him, but we are not sure. We left in such a hurry. Once I go back I will find out for sure," Dodor explained.

"Does she have blonde hair?" The blind Wanderer asked.

"Yes, how do you know that?"

"I have seen her in my visions several times. I am the seer of the Wanderers. Val is her name. She is very special. Unusual for a Flyer to have blonde hair. I will meet her, soon. She is a seer as well, a courageous one, not trained yet, but very gifted. There is even more to her, I can sense it, I can sense her. What is it?"

"I don't know," Dodor replied, irritated by those words.

"Blonde hair and wings. Only Wanderers have blonde hair." Mot leaned on her walking stick and stared with her blind eyes into the sky. She hummed absentmindedly.

"You have to warn your people that war is coming," Dodor said, trying to redirect the conversation. This seer Wanderer had confused him. "I know Wardor. He will want to control the Mountains and the Flatlands, and you know how he feels about the Wanderers. His mind is filled with revenge and hatred, but we have to follow our belief that we are all One People."

"One People, Dodor. That is what we believe in, too. But you know that among the Wanderers there are also warmongers and those who hate the Flyers," said Mot.

"Aldor will find a way to unite us," Dodor replied. "He has to, but we need your help."

"We will be ready," the man said, speaking for the first time. He was so tall and muscular that Dodor couldn't take his eyes off him. Dodor stared at the bear-like human. The man's voice was more a growl than friendly words.

"One of our women gave birth to a Flyer baby just four days ago. What shall we do with the Flyer baby now that war has likely broken out in the Mountains?" Mot asked.

"We will still be able to take the baby with us. Do you have her with you?" Dodor asked.

"No, but we can bring her tomorrow evening."

"I don't know. Do we have time to wait?" asked Dodor, looking at his two Flyers.

"We have to make time," one of them answered. "We can't risk the life of a Flyer baby by leaving it here. They have the same laws we have."

"So it will be then," Dodor said. "We will wait for you. Talk to your people and let us know what you plan to do."

"We will. Stay hidden. We will see you tomorrow evening." Mot replied.

The three Wanderers turned around and disappeared into the darkness. Dodor heard the baby protest slightly, but the sound faded away quickly and everything around them became quiet.

Dodor liked the Flatlands. For him it felt like home, peaceful and tranquil. He didn't know why, but he often thought about the idea of One People. He strongly believed in it. "Let's get some rest," Dodor said. "I will take the first watch." He sat down beside the fire the two Healing Flyers had made and thought about what might be happening at home. *Wardor is in control, unthinkable but possible. I can't return to the Five Mountains. If Walhalor has been declared, the only safe place is Ardar.*

The night sounds of the Flatlands started up — coyotes sang to the moon, owls hooted and looked for rodents, and Dodor felt like a stranger in a land that was strange yet familiar at the same time. He liked the Wanderers he had met so far, the ones who had the same values and beliefs the alliance held. He felt a connection with them. He remembered his grandparents always talking about the war and the hatred they'd felt for the Wanderers. "There can't be any peace between them and us. We have to revenge our ancestors," they used to say.

"Revenge for what?" Dodor had asked many times, but no one had ever given him an answer he could understand.

"Because they are our enemies," his grandfather had usually said. "They are different, and we hate them."

"But why do you hate them?"

No good answers, only hatred passed on from generation to generation. Hatred without explanation, even though there hadn't been any fighting between the Flyers and the Wanderers for the past thirty years. Many Flyers and Wanderers had grown up without knowing what war was like. However, there were always those who continued to warmonger and bring up the hatred that couldn't be explained. From what Dodor had experienced, the Wanderers were not much different than the Flyers in their hopes, wishes and values. They longed for a peaceful life with their families close by, to watch their children grow up, to celebrate their holidays and birthdays, and to enjoy colorful sunsets. They longed to feel the wind in their hair as the wind crossed the Flatlands or blew through the Mountains. The wind didn't treat them differently, didn't mind if it rushed through Wanderer or Flyer hair — it was there for everybody.

So why are there those who have to fight? Why can't they enjoy the simple things in life like love, family, and harmony — the things that are most important? I will never understand what goes through the minds of those lost in hatred, no matter if they are Flyer or Wanderer.

*** *** ***

The following day passed quickly and uneventfully. The three Flyers waited anxiously for the return of the three Wanderers. As the sun settled in the West, they finally returned with a baby Flyer in the arms of one of the women.

"Welcome back," Dodor greeted them. "What do your people say?"

"They are worried. Rumor has it that the clan knows what is happening in the Mountains. All I know is that the obvious is not always real. The Wanderers are preparing for war," Mot explained.

"What do you mean?"

"It is being said that Wardor is not only planning to attack the Wanderers, but is also planning to kill the Rescue Flyers. We will help you if you need us. You know the signal."

"Yes, thank you," said Dodor, panic in his voice. "How do you know?"

"The Elders among the Wanderers, those who believe in the One People, have a spy among the War Flyers. Don't ask me why, but I believe in their knowledge. Take good care of the baby, Dodor, Lord of the Healing Flyers, and good luck."

"I will keep him safe," Dodor said as he accepted the tiny bundle of blankets in which a small body moved. Dodor carefully moved the blanket aside and saw two friendly, brown eyes smiling at him.

"So innocent," he thought, with tears in his eyes. "Let's fly to the Mountain of Wind and deliver the baby. I have to find Aldor as soon as possible and bring him the bad news." Dodor wrapped the baby back into the warm blankets and carefully laid it in his harness.

The Flyers opened their wings and were carried away quickly by the flatlands' nightly breeze. As they flew away, a dark, threatening shadow emerged from behind a dead tree and watched the Flyers disappear into the dark sky. The moonlight shining across the flatlands touched the face of the Wanderer who stood motionless, looking into the sky.

"Good news for the clan," he whispered and walked into the night.

*** *** ***

Dodor and the two Flyers landed quietly at the edge of the Cliff on the Mountain of Wind. They sneaked through the forest, carefully and alertly crossed the Village of the West and ran toward Val's house. Without being seen, they reached the small cottage that stood at the end of a dark street. They had avoided several War Flyers who were patrolling the area.

"So, I was correct. A state of emergency has been declared by Wardor. Walhalor has been called upon. Did you see the armed War Flyers?" Dodor asked. "I hope Aldor is safe." He carefully knocked on the back door, but there was no answer. After the third knock, he heard nervous voices inside; a white face appeared at the window. The door opened silently and a woman beckoned, "Dodor, quickly, come in." As the door closed behind the three Flyers, the woman continued excitedly. "There is a curfew! What are you doing here so late? Walhalor has been declared. Most of the Rescue Flyers are in prison and the Council has been arrested. You and Aldor have been declared outcasts. You are being charged with treason. What is going on?"

"There is no time to explain, but Wardor is wrong. We brought you your son," Dodor said with a smile.

"So it is true, then." The woman started to cry. "My son is still alive. I couldn't believe it when the Healing Flyer told me." She carefully took the baby in her arms and held him close.

"This is not my son!" she declared suddenly. "So, Wardor is right with his accusations?"

"I am sorry, but you have to believe me. Wardor is out for revenge. Your son is alive. He was born without wings, and you know the law."

"Where is my son?"

"He is safe," Dodor explained, not really knowing where the baby was.

"You are a traitor then, Cousin. How is this possible? What do you want me to do? If Wardor finds you, he will kill you."

"Care for the baby, and please don't tell anybody," Dodor pleaded.

"As a friend, I will do as you ask , but I want my son returned to me. Whatever he is, he is my son. I see what you are doing, and I support you and love you for risking your own life. Be safe now and watch out. War Flyers are everywhere."

"Thank you. Take care of yourself."

"Val is missing. And so are Timo and Dino."

"Thank you for letting me know. Don't believe what you hear. Listen to the words but hear with your heart and make your own judgment."

Dodor and the two Healing Flyers quickly left the house. "To Ardar," Dodor whispered. "We must hurry."

CHAPTER THIRTEEN

Wolf

Wardor's plan had been executed well, better than he could have imagined. Most of the Rescue Flyers were in prison, and Aldor was on the run. Nevertheless, Wardor hadn't paid attention to the wolves and their courageous leader, Wolf. Wardor had never taken the wolves seriously. And he did not respect the Golden Eagle. To Wardor, having these animals on the Council was a mere symbol of harmony with nature, a gesture of goodwill, nothing more. He barely tolerated them at the Council meetings and had spoken openly against their presence. He had been overruled.

As soon as Wardor had declared himself the leader, Wolf had run to his pack in the forest to inform them.

"We must act according to our alliance and our values," Wolf told them. "The time of the wolves has come. We are ready."

"Do you think it wise to go against the lord of the War Flyers?" asked Ordar, a muscular, black wolf with glittering yellow eyes.

"We are not fighting the War Flyers, my friend Ordar," Wolf replied, "but we have to support those we respect and who are just."

"Why would we want to get involved at all?"

"What is happening in the Mountains affects us all. We will be drawn into any conflict, whether we want to be or not. In this time of great change, we must decide which side we are on."

"I am with you, Wolf," Ordar declared. "What does the wind tell you?"

"It tells that when the old stories came into being, the ancient Flyers knew their past, but now the past is forgotten. Some have written down what they know, but the new generation doesn't understand. The true meaning is lost to them. The Death Flyer will return to unite the two people. She will be called by the one who is of her blood."

The wind blew through the old trees and the leaves rubbed against each other, singing to the listening wolves.

"We are one hundred strong," continued Wolf. "It is late summer, the time of the Golden Moon that helps us find our way when all others are asleep. Ordar, you are in charge of organizing seven groups of six wolves each. Send a group to each of the Five Mountains so we can keep our ears on the enemy. We have to find the Elders and the imprisoned Rescue Flyers. Send one group to the headquarters of the War Flyers. We must find out what they are planning. Send the last group to the Mountain of Wind. A baby Wanderer is hidden there. Find the baby and watch over him. Aldor has asked for our help. Once you find the baby we must let Aldor know. The wind will help us with this.

"I will go to see the Spirit Wolf. She will identify the one who must ask the Death Flyer to return."

"You can't," Ordar protested. "It is too dangerous. You know what they say about the Flatlands and the big wolves that live there."

"You truly don't believe those old stories, Ordar?" Wolf asked, a smile crossing his muzzle. "Life is nothing but change in the midst of repetition. We must be ready for change, or it will overwhelm us. I will follow the signs of Mother Life. Don't worry, I will be fine. Please do as I say. It is very important we find out what is happening. You know the way of calling. The wind will carry your words to me."

"What about the rest of us?" asked a young grey wolf.

"You stay here, roam the forest and stay hidden. Be alert at all times, Midar. You are the leader of the young ones and soon will be called upon. Listen to Ordar. He knows what to do."

"Travel safely, my brother," Ordar said, knowing he couldn't change Wolf's mind. "May the Golden Moon guide your way tonight."

"I will be back when the moon is half empty. Be safe, my pack."

Wolf turned and ran into the night. He traveled eastward, toward the old hunting grounds and the falling waters. His grandfather had told him about the Spirit Wolf and where he could find her.

"When the time comes, you will know," his grandfather had said the evening he passed away. "The Spirit Wolf will be waiting for you near the falling water. She will show you the path you need to follow to bring hope to the Mountains. Nevertheless, be aware that with knowledge of your path comes pain and uncertainty. Once you know the way, you will realize how little you know."

For a long time his grandfather's words had made little sense to him, then Wolf had met the Elders who had invited him into their home on the Mountain of Glory. As Wolf ran through the forest with the wind blowing across his face and through his thick, grey fur, he remembered his first meeting with the Elders.

"Welcome, friend Wolf," Air had greeted him when Wolf had entered nervously the halls of the old stone library. Wolf recalled gazing up at the walls where the emblems of the Flyers had looked down on him." Please come in," Air had said.

Wolf remembered sniffing the air around him and smelling the scent of harmony, peacefulness, and trust — smells that reminded him of his pack. The three Elders — Earth, Wind, and Air —had smiled as they'd led the way into their meeting hall.

"Thank you for coming, Wolf," Air had said. He had told Wolf that they wanted to ask him to join their council. "You are part of the Mountains and thus part of us," Air had explained. "We would like to hear from you, and we would like to have input from you in our decisions. We would like to have your opinion."

"My opinion of what?" Wolf had asked skeptically.

"Your opinion about life, your opinion about the mountains, and your opinion about what the wind is telling you. We would like your opinion about everything. We need you to complete us. Your knowledge will help us understand life and the mountains better. Knowledge is never complete if collected by one, but together we might find real meaning. Sharing our individual knowledge can make sense of life and the mountains," Air had told him.

Those memories and words were vivid in Wolf's mind. The Elders had invited him into their home and had trusted him. It was his turn now to show them they were right in doing so.

"It is my time to return their trust. I will find them and help them." Wolf ran faster, elegantly avoiding trees, rocks, and bushes. The silver light of the full moon made it easy for him to find his way. He wanted to reach the end of the Mountain of Wind before the sun awoke to brighten another day with warmth and strength.

Wolf ran all night. By the time he reached the cliff in the east, the sun was traveling up the sky, coloring the horizon in a beautiful red and orange. Wolf stood at the edge of the cliff and looked down into the flatlands. The morning rays warmed his face; he saw the falling water and the old hunting grounds in the distance below him. He still had a long way ahead of him, so he rested a few hours below the roots of a fallen tree. In his dreams, his grandfather spoke to him. "I am proud of you, Wolf. You found your calling and you are strong. Tonight you will meet the Spirit Wolf. Not all that you hear will make sense to you, so remember why you want to see her."

Wolf awoke when Mother Life was high overhead. He stretched, yawned and bit into one of the many roots that surrounded him. Fresh water filled his mouth, so he tore off a root and chewed it hungrily. He had no time to hunt for fresh meat; a soft, nutritious root would have to do.

The path leading down the mountain into the flatlands was steep and torturous. Loose rocks, soft sand, thorny blackberry branches and slippery moss made the descent dangerous for most, but after several hours of navigating and balancing, Wolf reached the bottom of the mountain and the beginning of the flatlands without any problems. He was the lead-wolf of his pack because of his physical and mental abilities, because of his knowledge and experience, because of his character and maturity, and because of his wisdom and discipline.

He paused for a moment to smell the air and to listen to the wind. He heard the calling of his pack and knew they would be in position soon. He smelled the heat of the flatlands and sensed that no danger lay ahead. All was quiet and calm in front of him. Wolf began to run. His goal was to reach the falling water by nightfall. His broad paws carried him swiftly and quietly across the sandy land, with the wind by his side and the sun on his back. He loved to run on the planes without any trees, rocks, or bushes in his way. He felt free and unrestricted, and he took full advantage of this time alone. He ran as fast as he could, his paws barely touching the ground. It felt more like flying than running. Blood rushed through his body, into his muscles, giving him strength and power. Each stride he took was filled with determination and excitement.

"Yes," the wind whispered into his ear. "Run, Wolf, run. Feel free and do what you were born to do. Run."

By nightfall Wolf had reached the falling water. The mist filling the air provided welcome refreshment; he drank hastily out of the small lake. He felt strong and full of energy, ready to meet the Spirit Wolf. He was so excited he didn't notice the two, large wolves approaching quietly from one side.

"So you made it, Brother Mountain Wolf," one of them suddenly said. "The wind brought us the news that you were on your way."

"Welcome," the other wolf continued. They started to circle Wolf, sniffing at him and watching his every move with their crystal blue eyes.

"My name is Ganii and my brother's name is Nchaa. What makes you believe the Spirit Wolf will see you?"

"Nothing," Wolf answered carefully. The two other wolves were at least twice his size; he felt like a puppy. "I can only hope she will see me. The Flyers are in an uproar. Walhalor has been declared. I need the Spirit Wolf's advice and guidance."

"We are not interested in what is happening in the Mountains," Ganii replied.

"But you should be, because eventually what happens in the Mountains will befall the Flatlands as well. War is coming," Wolf said.

"War," Nchaa growled angrily. "Who would start a war?"

"Wardor, Lord of the War Flyers."

"You go now, Little Brother. Go back into your world that we don't want to know anything about," Ganii said bluntly. "The Flyers don't concern us." He stepped closer to Wolf.

"But, I can't . . . ," Wolf started to say, but stopped when the two Flatland wolves growled and snarled.

"No more words," Nchaa threatened.

"Enough," a soft, friendly female voice suddenly said. "Let me talk to our brother from the Mountains."

"But . . . ," Nchaa began, then continued in a more respectful way. "As you wish, Spirit Wolf," he said, bowing his head.

"Come, Wolf. I would like to hear what you have to say." A white, female wolf stood beside the falling water. Wolf walked slowly toward her.

"Forgive my two centurions. They can be very protective. Thank you, Nchaa and Ganii. I will talk with Wolf alone."

"As you say, Spirit Wolf," Ganii replied, "but we will be close by."

"Come, Wolf," the Spirit Wolf said. "Walk with me and tell me about the mountains and your pack."

The Spirit Wolf was almost as tall as the other two Flatland wolves, but she smelled nicer, and Wolf sniffed in her scent. He smelled trust and openness, bravery and strength, so he began to tell her about the Elders, the Council, the alliance, Wardor, Aldor, and Walhalor.

"My grandfather told me to see you when the time has come," he finished.

"So has the time come?" she asked with a smile.

"Yes. I feel it, I sense it. The Rescue Flyers and the Elders are in great danger," Wolf explained. "They need my help."

"What else?" the Spirit Wolf asked gently.

"In my dreams I have seen a Flyer among us, one with our eyes, with our nose, with our senses. The one who will save us and who is of the Death Flyer's blood."

"Yes," the Spirit Wolf whispered excitedly. "Do you know how we call him?"

"No."

"He is known as Quo-Qui, 'Swift Wind' in the old language. The one who talks with the wind, smells the air, and hears the ancestors. You know who he is!" the Spirit Wolf said.

"No, I don't. Please tell me," Wolf begged.

"He is the one who walked so freely into your forest to watch your puppies play."

"No!" Wolf shook his head and his fluffy fur shook.

"Yes. You sensed it then, and you know it now. You have seen him fly, you have heard him talk, and you have smelled his scent the same way you have smelled mine. What did it tell you?"

"Character, maturity, discipline, wisdom," Wolf said.

"Yes, like the Death Flyer."

"Why don't the Elders know?" Wolf asked.

"They feel it, but they don't understand it. They have forgotten. That is what happens when you don't believe in the Spirit Knowledge. We wolves know the spirits are with us, guide us, and help us. We listen to them because we believe and trust them. The Flyers are afraid of their spirits for some reason, thus the name Death Flyer. Also, they don't understand that this Death Flyer was a female. She was the first Flyer who could talk with the wind, the first who believed and understood. Her blood is flowing in Quo-Qui."

"So what do I have to do?" asked Wolf.

"You know it already, don't you?" The Spirit Wolf smiled.

"I think so."

"Well, then tell me."

"I will try to contact Quo-Qui. If he is truly the one, he will hear me in the wind, and with time he will understand."

CHAPTER FOURTEEN

The Navigator

Dino and the Golden Eagle entered the Cave of Vision; it connected through a narrow tunnel with the main cave of Ardar. White crystals grew from the ceiling and the walls. The light in the cave was bright and the air was fresh. A soft, green carpet was rolled out across the floor. Dino sat down on the carpet and took the four books out of his backpack.

"Now," he said, looking with big eyes at the huge golden eagle. "Please tell me about the Flyers. All you know, everything, the smallest detail, their beliefs, their values, and their fears. Everything you know."

"The eagles see life and the Mountains differently than the Flyers do. Your past has been filled with violence, mistrust, and division. You know the story of the one people, Flyers and Wanderers together?"

"Yes, I know it, but is it true?" Dino asked.

"Have you listened to the Wind of Life, Dino?" the Golden Eagle questioned.

"No," Dino answered sadly, lowering his head. "I don't have the gift. I can't hear the stories the wind tells."

"I am sorry. I didn't know. The Wind of Life tells us about all creatures, small and tall, strong and weak, brave and scared. It tells how the Flyers and Wanderers were once one people. What is most important for you to understand who the Flyer is you call the Death Flyer. Your Elders and Gildor have recorded their knowledge in the four books, including what they know about the past. But they no longer understand what the past is telling them."

"They know but they don't understand? What do you mean, Master Eagle?" Dino asked. He sat straight and listened intently to Eagle's words.

"Knowing is one thing, but understanding the importance and connections of events is another thing. For example, and this is not a criticism of you, a navigator knows about atmospheric phenomena, cloud formations, winds, and updrafts. A navigator knows about thunderstorms, cumulus clouds, and downbursts. You can calculate and predict to a certain degree the weather and flying conditions, but you will never understand the wind the way a Flyer, who has the gift, will know the wind. I am sorry, but that is the truth. The same with the Elders, they know the past and they know life as it is now, but they don't understand because they have lost the connection between the two, between the past and the present, they have lost the Spirit Knowledge. They don't believe any more. Out of fear and misunderstanding you call this Flyer we speak of the Death Flyer. We call her Qui Natch Ndee, which means Wind of the People."

Dino listened attentively. His legs were crossed and his hands were folded in front of him. He was amazed at Eagle's knowledge and wisdom.

"You know the four books based on your talent as a navigator," Eagle continued, "but to understand the past you must read them in the same way a Flyer who can talk to the wind would. You must be the link between the knowledge and the gift."

Eagle got up, stretched his golden wings and turned to walk out of the small cave.

"Come with me, Dino," he said. "I will show you what I mean."

Dino stood up and followed Eagle through the large cave and out to the top of the mountain where the wind rushed across the peak. Dino braced himself against the cold wind. It was filled with energy, ready to rip out anything that stood in its way. Dino leaned into the wind, his body shaking from the cold.

"Listen," Eagle whispered into Dino's ear. "Can you hear the wind talk?"

"No. What is it saying?"

"Can you feel the wind?"

"No, I feel cold," Dino muttered through his chattering teeth.

"Feel beyond your simple senses. You feel cold, yes, but what do you feel beyond that? Go inside your body and feel. The cold makes you feel alive, it makes you feel your body, and it activates your senses. Feel alive, be alive."

Dino shivered violently, but slowly he began to understand what Eagle was trying to show him. He felt the blood rushing though his veins and he slowly became alive. He had never felt like this before.

"You feel it, don't you?" Eagle asked.

"Yes, I do. I really do."

"Open your wings!" Eagle yelled, shouting louder than the howling of the wind.

"No way," Dino yelled back.

"Open your wings, slowly. Trust the wind and feel it. If you fall, I will rescue you, but trust the wind."

"No," Dino yelled.

"Do it. Now!" Eagle commanded.

Slowly Dino opened his wings. The wind took hold of him immediately; its invisible fingers surrounded his body and grabbed his wings. Dino fought the wind, fought for his life, the sweat of his effort forming droplets on his forehead.

"Don't fight it," Dino heard Eagle beside him. "Surrender to the wind. It is your friend. Let it take over. Free your mind of your fears." Eagle's words mixed with the howling of the wind.

"Surrender," Dino thought. "How does Eagle know I am afraid?" Suddenly, he felt it. The wind lifted him up slowly when he surrendered to nature's strength and force. Dino no longer felt cold; it was just he and the wind, like a dance between friends.

After they had returned to the Cave of Vision, Dino was still unable to speak. He felt overwhelmed by his experience. He had felt the wind for real for the first time. Before it was just the wind, something that existed, but now it was like being touched by the elements.

"What you have just experienced was a bit of what Timo feels. Now you might understand why he lives for flying. You know now what he understands, but it will take more for him to become the Flyer that he really is."

"You always talk in riddles, Eagle. Why is that?"

"For you it is in riddles, but soon you will learn how to understand. The wind of change is coming, and it will affect Timo the most. Be his friend and be by his side. Now try to read the four books again with your newly found appreciation of the wind. For some, wind is life."

"The wind of change. The wind is life," Dino whispered.

"Learn to understand the knowledge that has been passed on. The Elders don't understand, I don't understand. It is up to you, young navigator, to bring the two worlds together." Eagle looked at Dino, his eyes glittering with mystery.

After the Golden Eagle left, Dino looked at the covers of the four books.

"Let's start with the obvious and then go into more detail," he murmured. Dino was alone in the cave; there was no sound, except his own heartbeat.

"The names of the Elders have meaning. I understand Air, Earth, and Wind, but what does Gildor mean? He is Timo's father. They wrote down what they know. I should be able to understand. I already know about clouds, weather, storms, and atmospheres, so I don't need to focus on that. It is like what I experienced in the wind. If I had continued to focus on the cold, I never would have surrendered, and I never would have danced with the wind. I must surrender to the unknown with an open mind. It makes me grow and understand." Suddenly it made sense to Dino what the Golden Eagle had tried to tell him. He opened the book *Soaring* and read the first words written below the title. He understood them for the first time.

The Wind of the People belongs to everyone. She exists for you to roam in freely, to experience joy, and to soar unhindered. Know her and she will bring you peace."

Dino lay back on the soft, green carpet and stared at the bright crystals on the ceiling. He imagined again the mountain peak and felt the sensation of the cold and the wind touching his body.

"The wind," he suddenly whispered under his breath. "The Wind of the People. That is Qui Natch Ndee, the Death Flyer, the father of all Rescue Flyers. Know her and she will bring you peace."

He jumped up, feeling completely excited. He ran his fingers nervously through his hair, picked up a pen and paper and wrote: "The Wind of the People will bring us peace. The

Wind of the People is the one we know as the Death Flyer.
Qui Natch Ndee."

CHAPTER FIFTEEN

Found

Val's grandmother sat in her rocking chair beside the fireplace. A warm, crackling fire was burning. She held her grandson gently in her arms and quietly sang an ancient lullaby. The baby's eyes were open, and he was smiling. Oldar had fallen in love immediately with the baby Wanderer, despite the hatred she had for the Wanderers. She had lost her husband during the last war. He had fought in the Flatlands to prevent the enemies from advancing into the Mountains. She sang absentmindedly while dreaming of the past.

"Hear the wind that will bring you sleep
Wander in the mountains far and deep.
Remember the ones who have gone before you
While finding the way in your own soft shoes."

A wolf howled in the distance. Oldar stopped singing, stood up slowly and walked to the window. The night was darker than usual. She closed the curtains.

"Wolves in this area?" she wondered aloud. "They are far away from their home."

She walked into her bedroom and laid the baby down in the small crib, the crib Oldar's daughter had already slept in and in which Val had slept for the first five weeks of her life. The baby was deep asleep; Oldar was looking forward to a quiet evening. She was working on a new basket in which she would hold mushrooms. The storm season was approaching, the time for the big mushrooms to grow quickly out of soft, mossy ground. She was looking forward to scavenging through the forest, gathering her favorite food. Her life away from the village, deep in the forest, was lonely, but she preferred it that way. Since her husband's death she had avoided contact with other Flyers; it reminded her too much of the times she had danced with her husband, celebrated with him, lived with him. Her only visitor was Val who came often to walk with her grandmother through the forest, to talk about her dreams of becoming a great Flyer and to confide in her about visions, which scared her.

"You have the gift, Val," Oldar had told her, "but I can't help you with your visions. I have never heard about a Flyer who could see the future. However, the old writings talk about some Wanderers who had that ability."

"I am not a Wanderer! So why is it possible for me to have these visions?" Val had asked, concerned.

"I am not sure, my lovely grandchild, but you are special. Keep your mind open and seek for the knowledge of the past. You might find the answer there. Some believe in the one people. Who knows? Maybe it is true, but I don't believe in it."

Oldar sat in her rocking chair again and thought about Val, hoping she would come by again soon. She was weaving her basket and listening to the wind that hushed around her little cottage, the cottage her husband had built many years before. They had spent summers here together and had enjoyed the peacefulness and harmony so prevalent in this part of the Mountain of Wind.

Suddenly a loud knock echoed through the silence of the night and a threatening voice yelled, "Open up!"

Oldar trembled slightly. She never had visitors that late at night. She put the basket on the floor and stood up slowly.

Another knock shook the door and the voice boomed," Open up!"

"I am coming," Oldar replied. "I am coming."

She opened the door, not expecting any danger, but was roughly pushed aside when three, heavily armed War Flyers rushed through the opening.

"You live here alone?" One of the Flyers asked.

"How dare you push me aside and enter my house uninvited?" Oldar protested.

"We are at war, old woman. Walhalor has been declared. Answer my question."

"War," Oldar whispered. "Not again."

A quiet complaint came from the bedroom. One of the War Flyers rushed into the small room, his sword drawn.

"No!" Oldar screamed in panic and tried to run after him, but the other War Flyer blocked her way.

The baby suddenly began to cry as though it were in pain. "No! Don't hurt my grandson," she yelled.

The War Flyer returned from the bedroom holding the baby by one foot, its naked body dangling down from his massive hand. A disgusted frown crossed his face.

"A Wanderer!" The War Flyer announced triumphantly. "Wardor was right all along. You called this monster your grandson, old woman, old traitor."

"Yes," Oldar replied defiantly and proudly. "Yes, he is my grandson. Give him to me." She made an attempt to reach for the crying baby, but the War Flyer pushed his cold sword into Oldar's fragile body. With wide open eyes, she fell to the ground. The War Flyers walked out of the cottage and lifted to the sky.

"Wardor will reward us," one of them said, holding the baby tighter, making sure it did not fall to the ground. "The baby has to live so it can be offered to the Cliff. The old laws will prevail."

Oldar crawled toward the door and lifted herself up on the doorframe. She watched the War Flyers lift into the air and fly away, tears running down her weathered face.

Three pairs of yellow eyes approached out of the dark forest, and three wolves walked toward her. They smelled hatred coming from the human that leaned against the wood, and they smelled the death that was approaching.

They had watched from the forest after sensing a Wanderer baby close by. They had known right away when they had found the place they had been sent to watch. "We are too late," one of them growled. They ran back into the forest.

Oldar slid to the ground again and saw the Death Flyer approach. She saw bright, white wings taking her and lifting her into the sky. The last thing Oldar heard was the howling of the wolves; she suddenly understood what they were saying.

"Wolf," they howled. "The baby Wanderer was taken by the War Flyers, we were too late. Warn Aldor, the truth will be known. Death has come to an old Flyer."

CHAPTER SIXTEEN

Timo

Dino burst into the large cave where everyone was working quietly. They looked up, startled by his excited shouts. The Rescue Flyers, Aldor, Timo, and Val listened calmly as Dino told them what he had discovered. Aldor was pleased and said, "You are on the right way, but your path of understanding is just beginning. Be patient."

Be patient? Timo thought. *That is something I still have to learn before I truly understand the art of flying.*

The Rescue Flyers had built a simple table and simple chairs out of rocks and wood in the center of the large cave. They had prepared a small meal of bread, fruits, mushrooms, and salmon that was plentiful this time of year in the streams of the valley. All together they had a quiet, uneventful dinner, enjoying one another's company and the illusive peace.

Val and Timo spent the evening together walking and talking about Val's training. Dino disappeared into the Cave of Vision again. He had found the first puzzle piece and was eager to find more. He was determined to find the picture that would come from the assembly of all pieces.

Val and Timo's walk eventually took them through the small opening in the mountain wall where they stood beside the waterfall. They watched the endless flow of water and the rays of the setting sun that formed a small rainbow in the water's mist. Timo smiled.

"How do I find patience?" He suddenly asked.

"I don't know," Val answered, surprised by the sudden question.

"How did you find it?" Timo asked. "To be a true Rescue Flyer, you have to have patience or you might never be able to overcome the cold downdraft."

"But you did overcome it when you jumped from the Cliff."

"No, I didn't. Dino calculated the updraft for me. I doubted him, but he was right when he predicted the time the warm updraft would come. What about yourself, Val? Where do you find patience?"

"It is within me, and it is also within you. I did not have to find it. It has always been there. Yours might be hidden because of the sadness in your life. Maybe you have to learn to accept the things you can't change. It is easy for me to say because I haven't experienced the hardship that you have experienced, but maybe you could begin by not always feeling as though you have to prove your worth."

Timo looked into Val's eyes. Her words pained him and tears welled up in his own eyes, but he knew she was right.

"My father is dead," he whispered. He wanted to take Val's hand, but he was afraid of being rejected. "I can't prove anything to him, but I know I can do it."

"You are not alone, Timo," Val whispered into his ear. "You have many friends who are with you. I am with you."

He looked deep into Val's eyes and smiled. "Let's go back inside," Timo suggested. "I have to get up early in the morning and find something." He took Val's hand carefully and waited for a second. Val didn't pull her hand back. He smiled again, and together they walked back into the large cave.

*** *** ***

Timo's dreams were filled with strange sights of black animals with fiery yellow eyes and a large Flyer who descended out of the sky like an arrow. "I will meet you soon," he heard the Flyer say.

Timo tossed and turned in his bed until a hand touched his shoulder.

"Time to get up, Timo," Aldor said. "The updraft is soft and warm. Several storm structures are forming at the horizon. You know what that means, cold downdrafts on the rear flanks of the storms. Just the right conditions to learn about patience."

Timo felt tortured. His muscles hurt and his head throbbed. His back felt stiff and his legs were wobbly, but he got up and followed Aldor. It was a relief to leave his dream behind. He was confused about what the large Flyer had said to him in the dream. *The Flyer felt so real,* Timo thought.

When they stepped out of the cave and stood on the small ledge, Timo turned to Aldor and asked, "What is patience?"

"Patience means to wait for the right moment to do the right thing. It means thinking with a balanced mind, using all your senses, feeling your surroundings, and accessing your knowledge of what to do despite everything that is going on around you. Your gift allows you to listen to and to speak to the elements, but what you have to learn is to find your center, your most inner point of being. You must find strength and direction from the silence within." Aldor looked at Timo and saw in his eyes that Timo understood what he was saying.

"What you lack, Timo, is that silence," Aldor said seriously. "Completely letting go and trusting one's intuitive knowledge is what we call patience. I am sorry to tell you, but your mind is preoccupied with trying to know everything, trying to prove yourself. Free yourself of your father's shadow. He would have wanted for you to be free, to fly with the wind, to chase the cold downdrafts. He would have wanted you to be free to be yourself."

Timo stood frozen. Each word echoed in his mind. Each word hurt and made so much sense. Each word was true. Each word was painful. He didn't want to listen, but he knew that Aldor was right.

Aldor himself listened to his words and his pain grew when he thought about the cold downdraft, the icy claws of nature that had taken away his wife and son. He was still hoping to find them one day again, even though it had been many years since he had stopped crying when he was alone.

"Be myself," Timo whispered. "But who am I?"

"You will find out," Aldor replied. "You have the gift, but first you must become free. That is what your father would have wanted for you because he loved you with all his heart, for who you are and not for what you think you should be. By being yourself you will fulfill your father's greatest wish and greatest desire."

Suddenly the wind touched Timo's ear and he heard, "Your father is with you. He is inside you through your memories. Jump and feel him. Through me you will become one with him."

Timo looked at Aldor with a smile and jumped from the ledge.

"Follow me," he yelled as he opened his wings. The warm updraft caught him and pushed him past Aldor high up into the sky and into the clouds. Aldor jumped and tried to catch up with him.

Side by side they soared for a while. Their wings were open to the fullest and the wind came from below to support them. They glided through the air while Timo thought about Aldor's words. He felt as if a load had been lifted from his shoulders and from his heart. *Be myself,* he thought.

"Now you follow me," Aldor yelled, interrupting Timo's thoughts. Aldor turned to his right and flew toward a large formation of fluffy cumulonimbus clouds. Timo stared at the large formation towering high in the sky; this was the most unstable atmosphere he had ever seen. Large tower clouds were forming squall lines, which told him that strong, fast updrafts were rushing along the leading edge of the clouds, with even stronger downdrafts at the rear flank. Aldor was heading directly toward them.

"In the midst of total chaos lies a pattern of natural occurrences," Aldor instructed. "Let's see if you find your inner silence in that chaos."

As they approached the storm front, the wind gathered strength and the turmoil ahead of them expanded. The pair penetrated the lower clouds where they were hammered with hail and tornado-like winds. Timo heard the war song of the thunderstorm and was caught suddenly in a strong, cold downdraft. His wings were pushed back violently and he remembered his flight from the Cliff. He fought the same wind again as if his body were being ripped apart. Timo was thrown around, up and down, side to side, round and round and began to lose control He struggled and fought with the elements. Cold panic came over him. His mind raced, but he could think of nothing to help himself. Suddenly the elements overtook him and he collapsed. He stopped fighting and surrendered to the surrounding forces, at which point his mind became silent and clear. He felt at peace and suddenly understood what to do. He was no longer controlled by the storm; he was the storm. By surrendering to the elements he had allowed his intuitive knowledge to rise from the center of his spirit, the center of his patience. Timo saw clearly the pattern of the chaos unfolding in front of him, and he understood it. He saw the lines of the wind, the source of the hail, the direction of the tornado. His movements adjusted to the pattern in a way that gave him strength and control. He was no longer fighting; he was one with the elements. He remembered an old saying his father used to tell him:

One who attunes mindfully to the silence within can see and understand where one is and in which direction one needs to go.

"I understand," Timo yelled. "I found my center and my inner silence." He opened his wings and joined the howling wind in the wild ride of the thunderstorm.

When Timo and Aldor returned to Ardar, the sun was long gone and everyone was deep asleep.

"You did it, Timo," Aldor said with a smile.

"Yes," Timo replied. "I understood what you told me. The inner silence — patience. Thank you."

"Don't thank me. You did it, I just came along for the ride." Both laughed. "Let's get some rest now," Aldor suggested.

"I will stay out here for a while," Timo replied. "I am too excited to go to sleep."

"I understand. I felt the same when I found my center. Good night, Timo."

"Good night, Aldor."

*** *** ***

Timo sat down on the ledge, his legs dangling over the edge. He watched the many stars above. The storm and the clouds had passed and the endlessness of the universe unfolded in front of him.

"Timo," he suddenly heard a rough voice. "Timo, I have a message for you," the wind tickled his ear.

"Who are you?" Timo asked and the wind picked up his words and carried them away.

"So it is true, then. You can hear me."

"Yes, but who are you?" Timo asked again.

"I am Wolf, the Council member."

"Yes, yes, Wolf, I remember you. Where are you?"

"I am in the Flatlands where I met the Spirit Wolf. Are you safe? Where are you?"

"Yes, I am safe. I am at Ardar, with Aldor, Val, Dino, and the Rescue Flyers."

"I found out who you are. The Spirit Wolf revealed to me that you are known in the Spirit World as Quo-Qui, Swift Wind. I have to meet you. I have to see you. The Spirit Knowledge is within you," Wolf said.

"Where and when?" Timo asked.

"As soon as possible. I will . . . ." Wolf's voice faded away.

"Wolf," Timo said. "Wolf . . . ," Timo yelled into the wind, but there was no reply, only the wind singing its lullaby of endlessness and freedom. The wind actually teased Timo to open his wings again and let him be taken away, but Timo declined with a friendly "No, thank you, my friend."

Wolf's words echoed in his mind: *Quo-Qui, Swift Wind. What does that mean? I have to see Aldor tomorrow, first thing.*

*** *** ***

Timo's dreams were again filled with black creatures and fiery yellow eyes, but this time Timo knew who those creatures were. They were wolves, and Wolf, their leader, was standing in front of them.

Timo felt drained and tired when he woke up. The sun was still hiding behind the mountains in the east. His muscles ached and his head pounded. He felt something was changing within him but he didn't know exactly what was happening. He remembered the thrill of letting go and becoming one with the elements, the excitement of becoming the storm. Despite his pain, Timo jumped out of bed, dressed quickly and ran off to find Aldor. To his surprise, Aldor was already up. He and Dino were discussing some of Dino's discoveries.

"Come over, Timo," Aldor invited. "Join us."

"Sorry to interrupt you," Timo apologized as he approached, "but I have to talk to you before I go insane." Timo's mind was racing with all kinds of ideas.

"I am listening, Timo," Aldor said with concern.

"I talked to Wolf last night," Timo began.

"How?"

"His words traveled with the wind to my ears. He called me Quo-Qui, Swift Wind. What does that mean?"

"Quo-Qui," Dino interrupted. "I have read that before. It was in *The Art of Falling*, written by Earth, but it didn't make any sense to me."

Aldor looked bewildered. *There is more to Timo,* he thought. *Something is happening to him. His eyes, they are flickering.*

"Did Wolf say anything else?" Aldor asked.

"Yes, he wants to meet with me."

"Where?"

"He didn't have a chance to say. His voice faded away."

"We also need to talk about your experience in the thunderstorm. Do you want to talk about it now?"

"Yes, please. There is so much that makes sense now, and so much I still don't understand. I became one with the elements. I saw them, the air, the wind, the storm pattern, the atmosphere, and the structure within the chaos. As you told me, I let go and surrendered. I touched the deepest parts of my mind, my instincts and my intuition, my soul. Something awoke within me, something I don't understand. Wolf said I have the Spirit Knowledge. It is like an awakening. I see things that are not there. I hear things when it is silent. I feel things when my body is numb. What is happening to me, Aldor?" Timo's mind was racing faster than his mouth could follow. The words came out as if someone else were speaking them. He looked helplessly at Aldor.

"I have an idea. Follow me," said Dino while jumping up. "The answer might lie in Earth's book, *The Art of Falling.*"

Timo and Aldor followed Dino into the narrow tunnel that led to the Cave of Vision.

"Sit down," invited Dino once they were inside the cave. "The carpet is actually quite comfortable."

He took in his hands a thick book covered in red fabric and flicked through the pages. He looked at the summary page and whispered to himself, "I knew it, here it is, Quo-Qui - Swift Wind, Chapter Twelve."

He quickly turned the pages and began to read, "The identification of clouds plays an important role when predicting weather patterns and storms. Two basic shapes can be ... blah, blah, blah," Dino mumbled, then turned the page, mumbled a few more words and said, "Here, here it is: 'A rapid drop in pressure means a storm is approaching.' Makes sense, but now listen to this —

Quo-Qui, also known as Swift Wind, appears in the midst of the storm, at its center. Without him, the elements of time will overwhelm the people and the past will succeed. Quo-Qui will find a way to see the pattern in the chaos and he will unite the people who should be one. Thunderclouds are technically known as cumulonimbus clouds. High winds flatten the top of these clouds into an anvil-like shape. The anvil usually points in the direction the storm is moving. Qui Quo will face the storm and, with the help of Qui Natch Ndee, he will succeed."

Dino stopped and looked first at Aldor then at Timo. He suddenly sprung toward his friend. "Timo," he cried. "Are you all right?"

Timo sat frozen, his skin as white as the clouds. Dino touched Timo's shoulder slightly, and Timo fell backwards into the arms of Aldor.

"Timo," Aldor said fearfully. "Timo."

Timo's head hung backwards, his eyes wide open. He was barely breathing.

"What is happening?" Dino cried in panic.

"I don't know. Get some water and alarm the others. I will carry him to his bed."

Dino ran out of the cave. Aldor followed him, carefully carrying Timo in his arms. In the book Dino had dropped on the floor the pages moved, but no one saw what was written in dark, bold print on the bottom of the last paragraph of Chapter Twelve:

The shell must break before the bird can fly.

CHAPTER SEVENTEEN

Val

Val could still feel Timo's hand when she lay down in her bed. She had been surprised by Timo's show of affection towards her, but she was glad about it because she was fond of him. His hand had felt soft and warm, and firm at the same time. She'd felt her spine tingle slightly when she'd touched his skin. By his side she felt safe and comfortable. Nevertheless, these thoughts and feelings were quickly overcome by sleep, and her breathing became steady and regular. Her dreams appeared again, like they appeared every night. Sometimes they were just dreams, but sometimes they were a glimpse into the future.

When the moon stood the highest and was straight above Ardar, Val was tossing and turning in her bed. She saw Timo among wolves. At first he kneeled on the grassy ground and watched wolf puppies play in front of their den. Some of them approached him carefully and sniffed. Then, without hesitation, they included Timo in their play as if he were one of them. Suddenly, four male wolves appeared out of nowhere, growling and snarling with bared teeth. The puppies ran into their den and Timo slowly stood up. One of the wolves slowly moved closer to Timo. Six more wolves appeared. Timo stood still, waiting. He sniffed the air, cautiously watching the approaching wolf. Val continued to toss and turn; she wanted to help Timo. Sweat ran down her back as she helplessly watched the scene unfold; she was scared the wolves would kill her friend. She could feel Timo, but he was neither afraid nor scared. What radiated from Timo were pride and a sense of belonging. She saw Timo smile, and the wolf stopped in front of him. For a moment it looked as if Timo and the wolf were talking, but Val didn't hear anything. Timo turned his head and looked back at the puppies peeking out of the den. Without any confrontation or any more exchanges between him and the wolves, Timo walked away, leaving the wolf world behind.

Val woke up, gasping for air. At first she didn't know where she was. Eventually she was able to take a drink from the glass of water she'd placed on the floor by her bed. Her clothing, drenched with sweat, was stuck to her body when she got out of her bed.

"That was the past," she said to herself. "I knew about that story of Timo and the wolf puppies. This is the first time I've dreamt about the past."

She walked through the cave toward the small crack that led to the outside. When she stood on the ledge she was astonished by the beautiful sunrise. She turned her head to face the horizon where she saw huge clouds moving quickly across the blue sky. In the distance two Flyers were flying toward the forming thunderstorm.

"Aldor and Timo," Val said. "So Timo will meet the cold downdraft again."

She returned to the cave, hoping she would see Timo again soon. She missed his company and needed to talk to him.

The day passed quickly. Everybody was busy. The Rescue Flyers and Val practiced flight maneuvers and defense strategies. Dino was with the Golden Eagle, reviewing the four books. When night came and Aldor and Timo still hadn't returned, Val went to bed with worried thoughts and anxious feelings.

When the moon was high again, Val had another dream. A Flyer, dressed in the full uniform of the Rescue Flyers, stood beside a wolf at the Cliff on the Mountain of Wind. It was the same wolf that had approached Timo in her previous dream.

The Flyer and the wolf were talking to each other. "The time has come, my friend," the Flyer said.

"Yes. You are the one who will unite the One People again, but first you must find the one who is like you, but a Wanderer," the wolf replied.

"Will you go find your Flatland wolves and get ready?"

"Yes. I will meet you in the Flatlands again, Timo. Be careful." The wolf looked steadily at the Flyer then ran away toward the forest.

Timo? Val thought in her sleep. *The Flyer is not Timo.* Then the Flyer turned around and looked straight at her with Timo's eyes. "Timo?" she whispered.

Suddenly she heard the sounds of screaming and running. She opened her eyes knowing right away that something had happened to Timo. She jumped out of bed and ran to Timo's room.

CHAPTER EIGHTEEN

The Voyage

Timo didn't feel anything when Aldor laid him down on his bed. Val came running into the room just as Aldor was covering Timo with a blanket.

"What happened?" she asked hastily.

"I don't know," Aldor answered, his face as pale as the white feathers of a snow owl. "We were sitting in the Cave of Vision and he suddenly fell backwards, his eyes wide open, then he didn't move anymore."

She sat on Timo's bed and took his hand. Timo floated in a world only he saw, a world he didn't know. Strange beings moved around him, speaking in a strange language. Their bodies were transparent, more like outlines and shadows than real figures. It was as if Timo were in a large, white cloud. Dim light in various colors surrounded him. He could hear his father's voice. "Timo. Don't be afraid. You are exploring your inner silence and the depth of your soul. You are traveling through the world of your ancestors and you are guided by the spirits of the past. Just be and listen. Don't try to understand everything now. In time it will all make sense. We are from the same bloodline as Qui Natch Ndee, and you are the true heir of her legacy. You have the Spirit Knowledge which will give you understanding of the past and the present. Soon you will return to your world. Use this time to rest and listen to your inner silence. Find your patience and the understanding within you. I have to go, but I want you to realize that the real voyage of discovery does not consist of seeking new lands or mountains. Your voyage is to discover your mountains with new eyes."

Timo was suddenly alone. No voices, no movement; he rested peacefully. In his mind he soared across the Five Mountains, his home, but also traveled further, beyond the mountains, toward the Flatlands. In a long, sweeping circle he flew across a large town surrounded by old forests, freshly planted fields, and colorful orchids. He saw the marketplace in the center of the town where people were busy selling, buying, bargaining, and celebrating life with singing, dancing, and eating. He smiled and saw that the people lived together in peace, that the people were Flyers and Wanderers living side by side. Suddenly he felt a cold breeze and the scenery changed. He saw Wardor's face. He saw Wardor holding a bow loaded with an arrow. Wardor let the arrow go and it flew in the direction of two Flyers who stood near a dark, dead forest. When one of the Flyers cried out, turning as he fell to the ground, Timo recognized his father's face. An arrow had struck Timo's father in the back and had severed the main blood vessel in his heart. Timo yelled, his wings collapsed, and he fell from the sky into darkness.

*** *** ***

Aldor walked out of Timo's room into the large cave to get some fresh water. Timo had developed a fever and was sweating water faster than it could be replenished. Aldor stopped abruptly when a Flyer suddenly stepped in his way.

"Dodor," Aldor said, "my friend. Am I glad to see you!" He opened his arms and gave the lord of the Healing Flyers a strong hug. "Welcome to Ardar, my brothers," Aldor said, shaking the hands of the two Healing Flyers who had accompanied Dodor on his mission.

"We delivered the babies," Dodor said. "But I have bad news. We have entered a very dangerous time. The Wanderers

149

told us that Wardor is using the time of Walhalor to kill the Rescue Flyers he has captured."

"He wouldn't dare," Aldor protested.

"Why not? Before Walhalor he killed one of his own in cold blood," Dodor responded. "He is the law now. He will do whatever he wants to do. We have to expect the worst."

"I can't believe it, but you are probably right. What can we do?" Aldor asked, even though he already knew the answer. He knew Wardor was capable of killing the Rescue Flyers.

"Wardor must wait," Aldor said in a firm voice. "You are just in time. We need your help. Timo is not doing well. He fell into something like a trance and he has developed a fever. We don't know what to do. He may die."

"Lead me to him," Dodor said.

They walked quickly through the Crystal Hallway and entered Timo's room. He lay calmly on white linen. Val was by his side, changing the cold, wet cloths she had placed on his forehead and ankles to reduce the temperature that ravaged his body. Timo's face was pale and covered in cold sweat. Dodor walked closer and felt Timo's chest, then took his hand and felt his pulse.

"He is not in a trance," Dodor said after examining Timo. "He is transforming."

Transforming? Val thought. *That is what I felt when I touched Timo. My dream makes sense, now. I saw the future. Timo is changing.*

"It doesn't happen very often, but once in a while a Flyer comes along whose mind and understanding changes very rapidly. A very serious, mind-changing event usually precedes such a transformation. What happened to Timo?" Dodor asked, looking seriously at Aldor.

"I took Timo into a thunderstorm so he could become one with the elements," Aldor tried to explain.

"You should have known better, Aldor," Dodor said reproachfully. "You know about the old saying:

The Flyer who finds the elements will transform and his mind will be altered forever. Be aware of the consequences: either the Flyer is lost in his mind for eternity, or he will find the Spirit Knowledge."

"Why is everything written in a riddle?" Aldor asked angrily. "Why can't they just say what they mean?" He felt frustrated and upset, but he was also troubled by what he had done. *Dodor is right*, he thought. *I should have prepared Timo before taking him into the thunderstorm.*

"These are the old writings," explained Dodor, trying to calm Aldor. "At that time, all the words made sense. Be patient, my friend. Timo will awake again."

"But when? And then what?"

"We have to wait," Dodor replied.

"There is no time to wait. I have to act now. If what you told me is right, Dodor, then Wardor and his Flyers might have already begun killing my Rescue Flyers."

"We can't just rush into something and risk losing everything. Can you imagine a war among Flyers? That has never happened in all of the Flyers' history."

"You said that Wardor will kill the Rescue Flyers. We are at war already."

Aldor left Timo's room and called for his Rescue Flyers. They assembled in the center of the large cave. Dino came from the Cave of Vision and joined the assembly. The Golden Eagle was right behind him.

"The time has come to act," Aldor told his audience. "We are at war with Wardor and his War Flyers. Dodor has told me that Wardor is planning to kill the imprisoned Rescue Flyers. We cannot allow this to happen. We must rescue our brothers. War is upon us and we cannot wait any longer. We have to fight. We may lose our lives, but for me it is better to die while trying to rescue what is close to my heart than to sit and do nothing. Gather your armor and weapons. Let us fly."

The Rescue Flyers shouted in support and were ready to follow Aldor into war. They quickly dispersed to collect their weapons. It took them an hour to prepare before reassembling in the center of the large cave. Aldor returned dressed in his uniform; a glittering sword hung from his belt.

"My friends, loyalty and honor," Aldor said. "The time to fight has come." He raised his sword into the air. " Let us fly!" he yelled.

They walked toward the small crack in the cave's wall, but suddenly a dark voice echoed through the cave. "**No!**"

All went silent; everyone turned in the direction from which the voice had come. They looked into the firmly resolved face of a Flyer they knew and thought to be lost, but Timo stood strong and tall in front of them. Val was positioned resolutely by his side, looking at the surprised Rescue Flyers. Timo's wings were wide open and his muscles were tense. He stood taller than Val, his face stern but friendly, his hair jet black, his eyes sparkling and golden.

CHAPTER NINETEEN

Allies and Enemies

Wolf ran through the dense forest that surrounded the bottom of the Mountain of Clouds. On top of the mountain, Wardor's headquarters overlooked the Flatlands below. The night was dark and cold. Huge thunderclouds covered the sky and blocked out the light from the moon and the stars. All Wolf could rely on was his keen sense of smell, his sharp eyes, and his knowledge of the Mountains. He found the steep, narrow path that led up to Wardor's fortress, then followed the sound of a wolf's howling cry.

"Can someone stop that annoying howling?" Wardor yelled. "It has been going on for several nights now. What is wrong with those dumb wolves?"

"I have sent out several Flyers to put an end to it, but they have not returned yet," a small, shy lieutenant said.

"At least close the windows and put more wood on the fire," Wardor replied. "A storm is coming."

Wardor walked around the old, wooden table in the hall of his war council. Several of his lieutenants sat on comfortable chairs, waiting for their orders. Wardor had called them to inform them of his plan. The hall was dark. Only a few candles burned on the table; the flickering flames in the fireplace projected irregular shapes on the wall.

"Now that you are all here," Wardor began, "it is time to tell you about the next step. Our first priority is to get rid of the Rescue Flyers moldering away in the dungeon. We must kill them."

The fresh wood that had been added to the fire crackled; air pockets in the dry logs exploded with prickling pops. The lieutenants around the table looked at one another nervously. They were in shock and couldn't believe what they had just heard.

"Kill the Rescue Flyers?" a brave lieutenant asked hesitantly.

Wardor turned and looked at him angrily. "Are you questioning me?"

"No, my Lord, but aren't they our brothers and sisters? Our family?"

"Not anymore!" yelled Wardor. "They betrayed us. They broke our rules and disobeyed our laws. They are no longer family!" His face was red from anger and droplets of sweat formed on his upper lip. Spit hung from his mouth. "They are our enemies, and since we have them in our prison, the killing will be easy."

"We can't do that," said another lieutenant, standing up so abruptly his chair fell over.

Wardor smiled briefly, drew his sword, and thrust it into the War Flyer's chest.

"How dare you question me!" Wardor spat while looking into the dying eyes of the Flyer.

"Anyone else?" Wardor hissed as the War Flyer fell to the ground. Wardor waited for a few seconds, but no one else said a word.

"Good. I have made contact with the Wanderer clan and convinced them that the Flyers are having only a small family disagreement. I told the Wanderers that this dispute will stay among the Flyers and that they have nothing to worry about. They believed me."

"You have contacted the Wanderers?" a young lieutenant asked. "Isn't that against our laws, my Lord?"

"Yes, it is, but since we have Walhalor, I am the law now and whatever I do is lawful." Wardor wiped the blood from his sword and pushed it back into its sheath.

"The Wanderers have their spies everywhere and they know about Walhalor. Once we have killed the Rescue Flyers, we will begin our campaign against the Flatlanders. We will get rid of them once and for all."

"What is your timeline, my Lord? And how do you want to arrange your War Flyer troops?"

"Excellent question. Finally someone who understands. You tell me, my Lieutenants. Now that you know my plan, what are your suggestions?"

"Since we are entering the storm season, my Lord," the tall, dark-haired lieutenant named Palus began, "I would suggest that we do nothing for the time being except continue to listen to the Flyers on the Mountain of Wind. Find out what they think and how they feel. Walhalor has just begun and everyone is tense and nervous. Provide the Flyers on the Mountain of Wind with food, support, and comfort, and they will grow to trust and believe you."

"Just sit and wait?" Wardor growled, but he liked what he'd heard so far.

"No, my Lord. Watch and prepare. If we start killing the Rescue Flyers now, the Flyers will notice. Wait until the storms have arrived. Flyers get lost in them all the time, even Rescue Flyers."

"Hmm. What about the Wanderers?" Wardor asked.

"Infiltrate them and find out what they are doing and what they are up to. Will they just observe what is happening or will they prepare for war? Will they use Walhalor to attack us? Do they really believe you?"

"How do you suggest we infiltrate them?" queried Wardor as he began to pace the floor. He was intrigued by this young lieutenant and looked at him closely. He liked what he saw.

"Find a Wanderer family who is close to the clan but not too important to them. Convince the family to spy for you. I suggest that the threat of harming a young family member usually works well to convince a reluctant father or mother."

"Nourish my Flyers on the Mountain of Wind, spy on the Wanderer clan, make the Rescue Flyers disappear during the storm season. I like your plan. It is evil, but good. Find a weak Wanderer family and dispatch your Flyers. I like your ideas, Palus. I will remember your name, my friend."

Wardor looked at him for a long time; Palus stood his ground.

"Now you have heard me. Let's get going and prepare. The storms will come soon. This is what I say and what I've decided. So it is said, so it is done."

*** *** ***

Wolf continued to climb the steep mountain path for what seemed like half the night. By the time he reached the top of the mountain and Wardor's fortress, the wind had gathered strength and it had started to rain. Wolf avoided several War Flyers who were guarding the dark, threatening fortress. It didn't take him long to find one of his pack members. Findar, a grey wolf with crystal blue eyes, long fur, and broad paws, had been watching Wardor's stronghold for several days.

"Wolf," Findar whispered. "You made it. I hope you had a safe journey."

"Yes, thank you my brother. I found the Spirit Wolf and spoke with her. What news do you have?"

"Wardor plans to kill the Rescue Flyers and then attack the Wanderers. The plan is to wait until the storm season before they do anything. I think we call that season the time of the boiling clouds." He smiled and continued. "Those Flyers have funny descriptions."

"That doesn't leave us much time. Thank you, Findar. You did well. I have to talk to our pack and to Timo," explained Wolf as he trotted along.

"Be careful. War Flyers are on the hunt for us. Timo?" Findar suddenly asked. "Isn't he the one who walked into our forest years ago? The young Flyer we almost killed?"

"Yes," Wolf replied. "Why didn't we kill him?"

"Have you forgotten? It was the strangest thing I have ever experienced. He smelled the same as we do, and we felt as if he were one of us. You really don't remember?"

"Oh, yes, I remember very well, as if it were yesterday. I just wanted to find out what you remembered. That is why I have to contact him. He has the Spirit Knowledge. He is one of us."

Wolf disappeared into the night like the wind that blew across the mountaintops, invisible and quick. He had to find a safe place where he could communicate with Timo. The Spirit Wolf had told him that the time had come for Timo's voyage. Timo would need guidance once he'd completed his transformation.

CHAPTER TWENTY

Understanding

"Timo?" Aldor asked in disbelief. "How . . . ? How is this possible?"

"Timo met his ancestors," Val whispered as if Timo were still in a trance and she didn't want to wake him. "He went through his transformation as predicted by Dodor."

"I have traveled a long way," said Timo. His voice was deep and clear. "My ancestors confirmed that I am known in the spirit world by the name Quo-Qui. Wolf was right."

"Yes," Dino whispered. "Quo-Qui, Swift Wind."

"What else have you learned, Dino?" Timo asked, looking intently at his friend.

"The Death Flyer's real name is Qui Natch Ndee," answered Dino.

"Yes, Qui Natch Ndee means 'Wind of the People'. What else?"

"Qui Natch Ndee is the father of all Rescue Flyers and you are his direct descendant. In you flows his blood. Qui Natch Ndee has returned through you."

"Yes and no, Dino. You can't bring back the dead, but you can bring back their knowledge and learn to understand it. I represent her values, ideas, and hopes. Each of her values is explained in the titles of the four books you have read. They are discipline, maturity, wisdom, and character. Can you figure it out, Dino? I know you can. Think about it and let's meet later and talk further."

"You said her values, what do you mean?"

"Qui Natch Ndee is not our father, she is our mother. We have always talked about our father, never about our mother, but it was she who gave birth to the first Flyer and to the first Wanderer. That is why sometimes we don't understand the ancient writings. The one people came from the mother of all, from Qui Natch Ndee."

"I haven't understood one word," Dodor said. "All I see is that you have transformed into a magnificent Flyer, Timo. Your eye color is different too. Your eyes are yellow. Please let me examine you. Aren't you exhausted?"

"No, thank you, Dodor. I feel fine. I have to go. A friend is calling me and he has important news. Please excuse me and let me listen to the wind. I will try to explain when I return."

Timo took Val's hand and they walked through the cave to the narrow entrance and onto the small ledge. He looked at Val and both opened their wings at the same time. The wind engulfed them immediately and lifted them into the sky. Timo was one with the elements at once and Val noticed it immediately. She watched as the elements followed his lead and danced around him to his music. Where she was struggling and fighting with the wind to keep up, Timo was cradled by the wind and supported by the elements. He moved freely within the sky without restrictions. It was as if he were the sky.

They landed on top of the old mountain and sat cross-legged on the rocks. Timo closed his eyes and listened to what the wind carried to him. Suddenly he whispered, "Yes, brother Wolf, I can hear you."

"Quo-Qui, the Spirit Wolf told me about you and Qui Natch Ndee, but by now you know. You have the Spirit Knowledge, the knowledge of time, the present and the past."

The wind howled and Val moved closer to Timo. She was cold and shivered slightly. Timo put his arm softly around her shoulders and pulled her closer.

"My wolf brother told me that Wardor is planning to kill the Rescue Flyers," Wolf continued. "He will wait until the storms have arrived, then he will make them fly down the Cliff with bound wings. The storm season will soon be here. Get ready, my brother. You don't have much time. When you need us, we will be ready."

"I will call on you. Thank you, Brother Wolf," Timo whispered. The wind took the words from his lips and carried them swiftly to Wolf's ears.

*** *** ***

When they returned to the cave, it was raining outside and the wind had pushed thunderclouds into the mountains. Aldor, Dodor, the Golden Eagle, and the other Flyers were assembled around the table in the center of the cave, waiting eagerly for Quo-Qui's return. All of them were quiet, confused by the events and Timo's transformation. All except one. Dino had returned to the Cave of Vision and had reviewed the four books yet another time, with new information on his mind. He read the books again with a different perspective and he began to understand. He couldn't wait until his friend returned so he could talk with him.

"Timo," Dino yelled when he saw him and Val. He ran toward them. "I understand," he said to Timo.

Timo's eyes glittered dark yellow. In the darkness of the cave he looked like a dangerous wolf. Dino hesitated when he saw this and took a few steps backward.

"Don't worry, my friend," Timo said, noticing Dino's hesitation. "I'm still the one you knew from before. The one you invited to your house, the one you played with at school, the one who is your friend. My eyes are something to get used to. Let's join the others so they learn to understand as well."

"Welcome back, Timo," Aldor said wholeheartedly. He stood up and walked towards his friend's son. "I still can't believe what is happening. Welcome back, Val."

"Welcome, Aldor," Val replied.

"I can't either. Everything is happening so quickly, but I understand what is required of me. So, what have you found out, Dino?" Timo asked, turning his attention to his friend.

Dino couldn't hold back. It was like a waterfall of information flowing from his mouth. He was so excited he began to ramble.

"Hello, Dino," Dodor finally said. "Slow down and say it in a way we can all understand."

"Yes, sorry, yes I can, I'm sorry, I'm so excited, sorry," Dino apologized.

Timo smiled because he knew how Dino felt. He felt the same way.

"Okay, let me try again. Maybe you can help me, Timo. Ah . . . sorry, Quo-Qui?" he gave a quick look to his friend who stood supportively by his side.

"The knowledge of our ancestors has been passed on from generation to generation, but the meaning of that knowledge is lost. Over time our values and beliefs have changed, our people have changed and evolved, our thinking has changed, but the knowledge has been transmitted in its original form. Gildor and the three Elders have written it down in their books where, combined with their academic teaching and scientific explanations, it makes little sense to us. After I learned that the mother of all of us, known to us as the Death Flyer, is actually Qui Natch Ndee, Wind of the People, and that you, Timo, Quo-Qui, Swift Wind, are her direct descendant, I found the true meaning of the ancient knowledge."

Dino stopped speaking to take a sip of water from a glass that stood on the table. He noticed he had the full attention of everyone around him and they seemed to understand what he was trying to say.

"Without going into too much detail, the ancient knowledge is telling us that the Wanderers and the Flyers are one people." He stopped again to take a deep breath. "We all used to live together. We shared our villages and our food, we harvested and shared the land. Four virtues were highly important to our ancestors, virtues we have lost, and lost with these virtues have been our happiness and direction."

Dino looked at his friend Timo, who gave him an encouraging, agreeable, and supportive smile.

"Of these virtues the first is **Wisdom** — Know what you can change and change it, know what you cannot change and don't waste time trying to change it. As it is written in *The Art of Falling*: There will be a time when we all fall, at least once; the wise one knows that and prepares for it and is willing to get up again.

The second is **Character** — Do the things you promise to do even if the mood in which you have made the promise has changed. As it is written in *Severe Storm Structure*: Stay on your path and don't be misguided by what lies in your way.

The third is **Maturity** — Do the things that are just and don't find excuses for what is wrong. As it is written in *Cloud Lines and Rising Air*: In every chaos there is structure, as long as you stay true to yourself.

The fourth is **Discipline** — Follow through with what you have started. As it is written in *Soaring*: You must follow the cumulonimbus clouds, the epitome of the thermal in its most powerful form, to find your strength and inner silence." Dino looked into the shining eyes around him.

"Well said, my friend," Timo declared, "but what does it all mean? How does it all fit together?"

No one answered.

"To say it simply, we must find again the ancient values within us," Timo said. "Without them, we become divided and unhappy, like we are now. Wolf told me Wardor plans to kill the Rescue Flyers once the storm season has arrived. Wisdom, character, maturity, and discipline were the values of my ancestor Qui Natch Ndee, and they are my values. For now I must rest some more. I will see you in the morning. Learn more from Dino. Listen to your inner silence and patience and find strength in them. Remember, we are one people and it is up to us to unite all Wanderers and all Flyers. Get ready to rescue our brothers. Soon we will fly to the Cliff of the Mountain of Wind to face our enemy."

"There is more," Dino said carefully. "There is another message in the books. It says that to save the one people, you, Timo, have to find your brother."

"My brother?" Timo asked.

"Yes, your brother who lives in the Flatlands. It is written that the first Flyer gave birth to two babies, two sons, a Flyer and a Wanderer, when it all began many generations ago. There has to be a brother because together the brothers save the one people. Since Qui Natch Ndee is the mother of all, the first Flyer, she is the origin of the one people. "

"Is that all you have discovered, friend?" Timo replied.

"Yes, why do you ask?"

"There has to be more. What you've told me is what has already happened. What about the present and the future? What do we have to do to stop Walhalor?"

"I haven't found anything about that in the four books."

"Please look deeper. You know about Qui Natch Ndee, about Quo-Qui, about my brother and about the ancient values. Bring it all together and look for the plan," Timo concluded.

"I will do this," Dino replied and walked back into the Cave of Vision.

Aldor looked at Timo with amazement and admiration. He walked toward him and laid his hand on Timo's shoulder. "The storm of change has come, Quo-Qui, son of Gildor and Qui Natch Ndee. You are the true heir of all Flyers and I will follow you. Please take your place among us, Lord of the Rescue Flyers."

"Thank you, Aldor. I will take my place once we have found ourselves again. First we must prepare to rescue the Rescue Flyers and Elders. After that, we will begin to unite all our people."

CHAPTER TWENTY-ONE

A New Beginning

Timo entered his bedroom and lay down on his bed. He felt exhausted from the day and its events, but he also felt at peace. He had discovered who he was and had found his ancient values. He truly believed they were the key to three things: happiness, understanding others, and respect. To live united with all his people, he knew that respecting the wishes and ideals of others was more important than satisfying his own needs and wants.

When Val entered the room he smiled. She sat down on the edge of his bed and looked into his yellow eyes. She carefully, softly moved her fingers through his thick, black, curly hair.

"Sleep," she whispered into his ear. "You need your rest. Don't worry, I will stay with you."

"Thank you, Val. I like you by my side. It gives me comfort and strength."

Timo closed his eyes and sleep quickly overcame him. He drifted into a dream world filled with ancient creatures, storms, and pain.

Suddenly an old voice called for him. "Timo," the voice said, "Child of the Sky."

"Who are you?" Timo whispered.

"We will meet in the Flatlands, in the old forest, under the leaning, dead willows. I am a Wanderer, a very old Wanderer. My people call me Mot. I am the blind seer, but have lost all favor with the clan. You must know war is coming between the Wanderers and the Flyers. You must know there will be no winner. In times of darkness, evil will face good, but who will prevail?"

"First I must bring peace to the Flyers," protested Timo.

"I know, but a Wanderer walks across the Flatlands, a Wanderer who will be known as the Child of the Land. He will be there to help you when you need him. When he starts running, he will be ready. He is your brother."

"Where is he?" Timo shouted in his dream.

"Just remember, the Child of the Sky and the Child of the Land have to be together to unite the two people."

The dreams and voices stopped and Quo-Qui fell into a deep, healing sleep. Val watched as Timo's chest moved slowly up and down. She curled up beside him and joined him in the land of rest. Soon the dreams started for Val and her tossing and moaning woke Timo.

"Val," he whispered into her ear. "Wake up, it is only a dream."

Val opened her eyes and looked at Timo.

"No, Timo," she said calmly, tears filling her eyes. "These are not just dreams. What I saw was the future. A future I don't want to know."

"Please, tell me, what did you see?" Timo asked gently, noticing that Val was trembling.

"I saw you and a young Wanderer. He was your age, height and build. You were both standing among dead trees in a dark grove. Angry, shouting Wanderers surrounded the grove and threw their torches into it. The dead, dry trees caught fire right away and the fire raced through the grove with tremendous speed." Val stopped and look into Timo's eyes.

"What else?" Timo asked.

"Nothing," Val said sadly. "Just smoke and fire. I didn't see me. I was not by your side and the fire ate all the dead trees, then there was no sign of you."

They sat up side by side for a long time. Timo held Val's hand and thought about her words.

"We are in dangerous times, Val," Timo finally said. "I don't know how it all will end, but I know we will be together after everything is over."

"How do you know? How can you be so sure?"

"The wind will be with us all the time and it will connect us. I will always know where you are and you will always know where I am. Believe in it and believe in us."

Val smiled and gave Timo a quick hug.

"I believe in you, Timo," she whispered into his ear.

They lay down again and fell asleep quickly, comforting each other with their presence. The wind howled outside the cave around the mountain; it sang the sad song of desperate times and unnecessary pain. The wind had sung this song before, many times. Only one was listening to it and understanding it these days. However, for now that one Flyer was asleep and preparing to overcome the wind of war.

*** *** ***

The doors to Wardor's bedroom swung open violently and Palus walked in.

"How dare you wake me so recklessly. I will have your life for this," Wardor bellowed.

"Forgive me my Lord, but once I have told you what has happened you will thank me," Palus explained while kneeling on one knee, his head bowed low.

"Tell me, quickly, so I stop my sword before it cuts your head off."

"Three War Flyers have just returned from the Mountain of Wind and they bring you a present."

"Don't tempt my patience, you fool. What did they bring?" yelled Wardor. He held his sword high above Palus's head.

"They bring you a baby, a Wanderer baby, found with a Flyer on the Mountain of Wind."

Wardor lowered his sword, it almost fell out off his hand. He stood as if hit by lightening, unable to speak.

"My Lord?" Palus asked.

"Where are those Flyers and the baby? I have to see for myself."

"Follow me, my Lord."

Wardor quickly pulled on his pants and shirt and followed Palus through the dark, cold hallways.

"You did right in waking me, Palus," he said, smiling.

Palus opened the door to the Hall of War and let Wardor enter first. Three War Flyers stood beside the fireplace. When Wardor entered they turned around and bowed their heads.

"My Lord," they said simultaneously.

"Where is the baby?" asked Wardor excitedly.

"It lies in the chair," one of the Flyers replied and pointed to the large, red chair standing in the center of the room. "I could no longer bear to hold the creature."

Wardor walked hastily to the chair and lifted up the almost lifeless baby. He turned it over and looked at its bare back.

"No wings," he announced. "Is it dead?"

"I don't know. It stopped crying when we reached the fortress."

"Well done you three. I will reward you well for that. Now go get food and wine to celebrate." Wardor looked triumphantly at Palus. "This is my proof," he said, holding the lifeless baby up high.

"It would be better if the baby were alive," Palus said.

"Why?" Wardor growled.

"If it is alive, you can offer it to the Cliff tomorrow and wipe out any doubt still lingering in some Flyers' minds.

Remember, they have to believe in the old laws, they have to support you and Walhalor. Give me the baby."

"Here, take it," Waldor said roughly. "You are more devious than I am. Save the baby, feed it and wrap it in warm blankets. Call for a spectacle at the Cliff tomorrow at noon. I will make sure the old laws are held in high regard."

Palus took the baby carefully and placed his ear on the baby's chest. The tiny heart was still beating but the flesh he touched was very cold. He walked out of the Hall of War and rushed down two flights into the servants' quarters. He knew a young Flyer there who had knowledge in healing and herbal medicine. He found her in her room and handed her the baby. "Look after the baby and get it well for tomorrow," he demanded. "If it dies, you will die as well. Don't ask any questions, just make sure the baby stays alive."

He left the room and walked to the mess hall where he commanded three lieutenants to fly to the Mountain of Wind first thing in the morning. They were to announce that a Wanderer baby had been found on the Mountain of Wind and that the Flyers of the mountain were to come to the Cliff to witness the old law being carried out. At noon, a baby would be offered to the wind.

Palus left the hall and walked to his bedroom. He was tired and exhausted by the events of the day. Things had happened which disgusted him. He had to find new strength in the darkness so he would be able to continue. His beliefs were different from Wardor's beliefs.

CHAPTER TWENTY-TWO

The Cliff

It was still dark when Timo woke up. He had heard a familiar voice call to him. He walked out of the cave and flew up to the Old Mountain.

"I am here, Wolf," he said into the wind. "What news do you have?"

"They found the Wanderer baby on the Mountain of Wind in the old forest," Wolf said. "Wardor will offer the baby to the wind at noon."

"Where?" Timo asked.

"The Cliff," Wolf answered.

"The Cliff," repeated Timo, and a cold shiver ran down his spine, the Cliff he had jumped off a few days before, where he had almost lost his life.

He returned to the cave and sneaked back to his room. He looked at Val, wanting to wake her, but decided against it. *She wouldn't be much help,* he thought. *She would only worry and blame herself.*

He turned around and walked back to the cave's entrance. He stepped out on to the ledge to find Aldor waiting for him.

"You can't go alone," Aldor said.

"I have to and you know that. If the baby dies, Val will die. She could never forgive herself. I am the only one who might make it in time to reach the Cliff."

"I heard Wolf. The offering will be at noon. I will come," Aldor insisted.

"No, you can't. If something happens to me, you have to lead the Rescue Flyers into war. You have to rescue our Elders and brothers."

Aldor didn't reply, he just looked at Timo with tears in his eyes.

"The wind will be with you, Timo. Strength and honor," said Aldor.

"Strength and honor, Aldor. Listen to Dino and plan the rescue. I will return."

Timo jumped off the ledge and opened his wings. The wind greeted him enthusiastically and lifted him up high. He rose above the clouds quickly and the wind sang into his ears, "Welcome back, Child of the Sky. I am pleased to hold you in my arms."

"Welcome, my friend," Timo replied. "Be on my side and support me well. I will need you and your updraft."

Timo folded his wings close to his body and shot toward the Mountain of Wind. Faster and faster he flew as he watched the sun rise in the east and travel slowly toward the south. Time flew by as quickly as he raced above the Old Mountains, and Timo wasn't too sure where he was when the sun reached its highest position in the sky.

*** *** ***

The crowd had begun to grow at a steady rate since early morning. By the time Wardor arrived, all the Flyers from the Mountain of Wind had gathered at the Cliff to watch what was to come. Wardor landed slowly. He was dressed in his war uniform, complete with bow and arrows fastened across his back and his heavy sword dangling from his belt. He was followed by at least eighty War Flyers. One of them carried a white bundle in his arms.

"Welcome, my friends," Wardor greeted the crowd. "Thank you for coming. I promised that I would be truthful to you and today is the day I will prove to you I must be believed. A baby

Wanderer was found on the Mountain of Wind. It was harbored by a Flyer who lived in the dark forest. When some of my brave and resourceful War Flyers discovered the baby they were met with resistance and had to fight for their lives."

A roar went through the crowd and one Flyer said, "The old witch, I knew she was playing an ill game."

Wardor signaled to the Flyer who was holding the white bundle. The Flyer stepped forward and opened the white blanket, taking out a baby without wings. He lifted it high above his head and the crowd screamed in awe.

"So it is true," some of them shouted.

"Yes, my friends," Wardor yelled. "It is true. The Elders and the Rescue Flyers have betrayed us for many years now, and here is the proof." Wardor pointed at the baby.

"All of you know the old law:

Those born without wings have to prove they are worthy to live in the Mountains. Take them to the Cliff and offer them to the wind. If they were meant to fly, they will return.

"Today we will honor that law and thus honor our ancestors who have fought so bravely and have given their lives so we can live in peace. Today we will offer this baby to the wind."

The Flyer who held the baby turned around to face the Cliff, sweat forming on his forehead. He looked down into the Flatlands and saw a cloud that had formed along the mountain face. In the distance he saw the sparkling blue lake and the yellow steppe that opened up wide in the land below. He hesitated. Never before had he taken a life; he was horrified with what he was about to do. It was his duty to follow orders, no matter if he believed in them or not. It was demanded of him to follow without questioning. He bent his arms slightly then lifted them abruptly, throwing the baby in the air toward the abyss. A tiny cry was heard as the baby fell.

A few Flyers screamed, a few Flyers cried silently, and a few Flyers looked away in disgust, but nobody stood up to confront Wardor. Everything became quiet as everybody waited, everyone knowing that the wind would not return the baby.

A hissing sound passed by the Cliff and a shadow crossed in front of the sun, but nobody paid it any attention. All had lowered their heads. Suddenly Wardor lifted his head and said, "So it is done, and so it is written down. War is upon us and we will find and punish those who've betrayed us."

He turned around and lifted into the sky, his War Flyers following close behind him. They flew toward the fortress that stood dark and monstrous on the clouded mountain.

*** *** ***

A hand stretched forward and strong fingers wrapped around the tiny leg of the falling baby. Suddenly, appearing from the white cloud that lingered along the walls of the Cliff, the cold downdraft opened its claws and wrapped itself around the forward rushing Flyer.

"So you've returned," the downdraft hissed. "Didn't you learn anything?"

"Oh, I did," the Flyer replied and opened his muscular wings despite the restriction of the merciless claws. The Flyer pulled the baby closer and held it tightly to his chest.

"I see," the downdraft said. "You've learned a lot, Child of the Sky, but not enough. You are too late."

Timo looked down at the ground that was rushing toward him. He opened his wings and soared gracefully upward towards the sky, holding Val's brother securely in his arms.

"No, I am not," Timo replied proudly. "Now I am stronger than you are!"

— The End of Book One —

ACKNOWLEDGEMENTS

I would like to thank Anita who stands by my side, strong and solid. She never doubted me, and she helped me keep my sanity when my head was in the clouds or my mind was in the flatlands. Her patience and understanding is admirable.

Chantel, thank you for your ideas and feedback. Your talent and imagination is very valuable to me. I cherish every moment we spend together.

Samantha Starkey, thank you for your time and genial input, and for your thoughts about the characters and the story. You helped me make this story so much better.

Calum Macdonald, thank you for your review and evaluation about the Mountain World and the Flatlands. Your ideas and thoughts made this story so much richer.

Marjorie Dunn, you are the best editor anyone can ask for. You helped me create a world on paper that exists so vividly in my mind. Your talent is so alive in the plays and musicals you have produced and was so overwhelmingly present during this project.

Accurance Group, thank you for making this dream come true. I can't praise your professionalism and enthusiasm enough. Your cover design is fantastic and the book layout is stunning. Thank you for producing this story and for your help making it available in print and in e-book format.

Preview: Book Two

The Wind Of Life
The Wanderers

There was a time when the difference in appearance among the people did not matter. They were one with each other and their world. Why can't people live in peace and build on the differences that exist? Is it so difficult to accept without criticism, to love without conditions, to understand without doubt, and to listen without interrupting? Watch the horizon, where sky meets land, and you will find the future.

From the ancient book
of The Wanderers,
Author Unknown

CHAPTER ONE

Run

Rider liked the calm and peace of the lifeless Willow Grove. No bird would ever sing here, no deer would ever give birth in this dark place, and no rabbit family would ever build their den among the dead roots. The forty willows standing lonely and wrathful on the flatlands in the middle of nowhere had been dead for many generations. This was a haunted place, a forgotten place, a doomed place, but for him it was like the home he didn't have, somewhere he was protected and loved by an invisible family that was hiding and watching from the leafless branches. Nobody told him what to do here; in the grove *he* was in control of his life and future.

After receiving a scolding or a beating Rider always found excuses for his father, even though he had long ceased admiring or respecting the man. *My father, the clan leader*, he used to think. *He is a very important man, a very busy man, too busy to waste time with his son. I have deserved the beatings, but I hate it when he calls me 'stupid' or 'idiot'. I would rather feel the sting of his hand swiping across my face. At least that pain will go away.*

He leaned against one of his willow wraiths.

"I am not stupid!" he yelled suddenly, but his frustration was absorbed quietly by the emptiness surrounding him.

Anger grew within him when he thought about his father. He pushed away from his tree and kicked it, hard. Black, brittle bark broke loose from the trunk, flying in all directions. A hollow groaning bellowed through the grove.

"I am sorry," he said quietly, remorsefully.

"Who are you talking to, Rider?" a frightened but sweet voice asked. "Let's get out of here. I don't like this ugly place, it gives me the creeps!" The little girl walked over to her older brother and grabbed his hand, shivering slightly.

"But you said you wanted to come and see the grove, Pai."

"Yes, I know, but that was yesterday, when we were at home. All these dead trees. Why do you like it here so much?"

Rider felt the growing fear in his ten-year-old sister. Her warm hand was sweaty and it twitched nervously, so he held it more tightly to reassure her that she was safe with him.

"Well, let's go then," he said suddenly and broke into a run, dragging Pai behind him. They ran for a few minutes, but when they reached a small hill that stood in the warm sun she yelled, "Stop! You run too fast. I can't keep up."

Rider stopped immediately and let go of Pai's hand. Breathing heavily, Pai collapsed on the soft, green grass, then lay back and closed her eyes. The warm sun tickled her body gently and soon the dark, cold place was forgotten. A soft breeze moved the grass and played with Rider's black, curly hair. He stood beside his sister with his green eyes focused on the black spot in the distance — his hideout, his home.

See you tomorrow, he thought.

"Tomorrow is the big hunt, Rider," Pai's voice interrupted Rider's thoughts. She had opened her eyes and was watching the clouds in the sky, trying to see if she could find creatures in the funny-shaped puffs of cotton.

"Are you ready to join the seventeen-year-olds on the first hunt? At fourteen you're the youngest boy ever to take part in this special event. Father is mighty proud."

"Is he?" Rider shook slightly as if cold water were being poured down his back.

"Yes, why shouldn't he be? The clan chief's son will beat out the seventeen-year-old boys for the biggest kill."

"Thanks, Pai," hissed Rider sarcastically. He was looking at her angrily.

"Thanks for what? What have I said?" Pai sat up and looked at her brother. She loved him, like a younger sister would love her older brother who is kind and understanding.

"Raising expectations! Putting on the pressure! Tomorrow is my first group hunt. I hate killing animals. When I went with father he would do the killing. Have you ever heard the screams of a fatally wounded hare?"

"Animals don't feel pain," Pai replied.

"Yes they do. They feel as much pain as you and I do. They feel joy when they taste fresh, healthy grass, they feel love when they see their young ones play, they feel happiness when they rub noses with their mate, and they feel pain when they die."

He looked at her with sad eyes. "I can still hear the screams," he added. "They haunt me at night when it is dark and quiet. The hare screamed for his family and wished them farewell and warned them about the hunter. I heard the pain in those cries and I stood there overcome with sorrow until Father broke the hare's neck and the screaming stopped."

Silence.

Pai had stood up and was looking at her brother whose green eyes were shimmering in the bright sun. Tears ran down her face. She could feel the pain of the hare and she could sense her brother's sorrow. Everything was quiet around them except for the breeze that rushed by Pai's ear and the beating of her heart. Never had she seen her brother so emotional and empathetic. She watched as a lonely tear ran down his cheek.

"That day will always be with me. I remember the smell. Freshly picked mushrooms, like the ones we used to pick in the autumn, down by the creek below the birch trees," Rider said, breaking the silence.

"But you hate mushrooms."

"Yes, ever since that day."

"I'm glad I'm not an antelope," Pai said suddenly.

"What do you mean?" Rider asked, irritated.

"The girls in my class say that antelopes must be the most heartless creatures in the Flatlands. If one of their young ones gets killed by a predator, they run away and just continue to eat again."

Rider's face turned red in anger. He stomped his foot and was ready to yell at his sister, but when he looked into her brown eyes and surprised face he calmed down. *How could she know?* he realized.

"The antelopes cry at night when the predators are asleep," he explained patiently and gently. "That's when they can let their guard down. That's when they show their emotions. You can hear them during the night, crying," he continued slowly, selecting each word carefully. "They have no chance to grieve during the day or they might fall prey to those who feed on them. We are the heartless ones, Sister, not the animals."

"Why do you defend the animals? And how do you know all this, or are you making it all up?"

"I feel what the animals feel, I hear what the animals say, I smell what the animals smell. When I wander through the silent night, I can hear them, I can sense them."

"You scare me sometimes, Rider. You are weird, you know that? I think what you need is a girlfriend."

Rider looked at her, confused, running his fingers through his hair.

"You're blushing," Pai yelled excitedly. She jumped up and down and ran circles around her brother.

"Stop that," Rider shouted. "You're making fun of me."

"No, I'm not. You just take yourself too seriously sometimes. Lighten up and be like the other boys."

Suddenly she stopped and the laughter in her face changed to frowning. She lifted her right hand and pointed to the mountains in the North.

"Look, Rider, look," Pai said, her voice trembling. "Thunderclouds. Are the brutal, deadly War Flyers coming again?" She grabbed her brother's arm with both hands and hid behind his back.

"No, dear Pai," he said softly, pulling his sister in front of him, stroking her brown hair gently.

"How can you tell?" Pai moved closer to her tall, strong brother, seeking more comfort.

"The clouds are grey and dark. When the War Flyers come, the clouds turn red. Have you been listening to the Elders' old stories again?"

"Why do the Elders hate the Flyers so much?" Pai asked.

"I don't know. Nobody knows. Nobody really remembers, they are just old stories."

"Scary stories. Like your stories. They are filled with anger and killing, hatred and dying, darkness and crying. The Elders said that the Flyers are evil and that they tried to kill the Wanderers. They killed some of our ancestors."

"How do they know? They might never have seen a Flyer. Who knows, maybe the Flyers don't even exist anymore," Rider suggested.

"It is written in the Old Book. They talk about the past at school, in history class. Don't you know that?"

"Yes, I know, but who says that all that is written is true? Who knows what really happened?"

Rider looked at the mountains and the large stack of cumulus clouds that had formed on the west side of the highest peak. He was intrigued by the thought of hiking up the Five Mountains and into the world of clouds in the hope of finding the Flyers. He didn't believe in the old stories, and the animals didn't believe in them either. Yet, he wanted to be certain, and he knew that his hideout, the haunted place of the dead willows, held some answers to his many questions.

"We have to go home, Rider," Pai suddenly said. "I'm scared."

"Let's run with the antelopes," Rider suggested. "You always like that. Let's see if we can keep up with them."

A relieved smile crossed Pai's face. She pushed her brother away, turned around and started to run.

"Hey!" yelled Rider. "That's not fair!"

He leaned forward and was off in a second. Pai was fast. Dust and small stones were hurled up into the air by her small, quick-moving feet. However, Rider was faster and caught up with her very quickly. He raised his right arm and pointed westward, in the direction of the open steppe of the flatlands where he saw a small group of antelope. The two quickened their pace and raced toward the grazing animals. Suddenly one of the antelope raised its head and whistled. The group of animals sprang up and ran away from the two fast-approaching Wanderers. Rider was the first to catch up with the fleeing herd and he yelled for joy. His high-pitched yelp washed across the dry land as he ran alongside the lead animal with blinding speed and long strides. His heart quickened; he was filled with unimaginable energy and happiness. Rider was in his element. He could run for hours without getting tired. He looked into the brown eyes of the lead animal and was surprised to see no fear in them, only mutual respect. The animal blinked and took a sharp turn to the right, leaving Rider running in the wrong direction.

Rider stopped abruptly and smiled. He was breathing evenly and calmly. Suddenly he noticed that his sister was far behind. When she finally caught up with him, she said breathlessly, "You are too fast, way too fast. You were as fast as the antelope." She tried to catch her breath. "How is that possible?"

Rider just looked at Pai and shrugged his shoulders. He put his arm around his sister and said gently, "I don't know, but we have to leave for home now so we can reach the village before it is dark. Come, let's run."

"But not so fast," Pai protested, though Rider was already on his way, at a more leisurely pace this time.

When Pai had caught up and was keeping pace alongside Rider, Rider reminded his sister, "I have to get up early tomorrow morning. You know what Father is expecting from me."

Dark clouds loomed on the horizon like the dark thoughts that arose in his mind when he thought about the hunt.

— Book Two will be available in November 2011 —

CPSIA information can be obtained at www.ICGtesting.com
Printed in the USA
LVOW030341191011

251067LV00004B/6/P